— A BIBLE STUDY FOR TEEN GIRLS

W9-APK-023

WE SAVED YOU A SEAT

Finding and Keeping Lasting Friendships

(in)courage community manager

LISA-JO BAKER

LifeWay | Girls

LifeWay Press® Nashville, Tennessee

Published by LifeWay Press® • ©2017 DaySpring Cards, Inc.
Reprinted June 2017, Sept. 2017, Nov. 2017

Author is represented by Alive Literary Agency, 7680 Goddard Street, Suite 200, Colorado Springs, CO 80920, www.aliveliterary.com.

ISBN: 978-1-4300-6400-8
Item 005791569
Dewey Decimal Classification Number: 248.83
Subject Heading: RELIGION/ Christian Ministry/ Youth

Printed in the United States of America

Student Ministry Publishing
LifeWay Resources
One LifeWay Plaza
Nashville, Tennessee 37234-0144

We believe that the Bible has God for its author; salvation for its end; and truth, without any mixture of error, for its matter and that all Scripture is totally true and trustworthy. To review LifeWay's doctrinal guideline, please visit www.lifeway.com/doctrinalguideline.

TABLE OF CONTENTS

ABOUT THE AUTHOR

LISA-JO BAKER has been the community manager for *www.incourage.me*, an online home for women all over the world, for nearly a decade. She is the author of *Never Unfriended* and *Surprised by Motherhood*, as well as the creator of *The Temper Toolkit*, and her writings have been syndicated from New Zealand to New York. She lives just outside Washington, DC, with her husband and their three very loud kids, where she connects, encourages, and champions women in person and through her blog, *lisajobaker.com*. She is convinced that the shortest distance between strangers is a shared awkward story, and she'd love to connect with you on Twitter, Facebook, or Instagram @lisajobaker.

(in)courage

FIND YOURSELF AMONG FRIENDS

At (in)courage you are welcome to a place of faith, connection, and friendship, where you will always find yourself among friends. Founded in 2009 by DaySpring, the Christian products subsidiary of Hallmark Cards, Inc., the vision for (in)courage was to create a new home for the hearts of women, where women take turns pulling up a chair to share their stories of what Jesus looks like in their everyday, gloriously ordinary, and often messy lives. Since then, (in)courage has grown into a vibrant community that reaches thousands of women every day, welcoming them just the way they are, offering a space to breathe, loving support, and resources for meaningful connection.

HOW TO USE THIS STUDY

Over seven weeks, this resource will lead girls through an in-depth study of friendships. Together we will unpack seven practical ways to take Jesus up on His invitation to love other people—to be friends who go first, who make the first move, and sometimes the hundredth move of starting over. To figure out how to get along with the people we love, as well as the ones who rub us the wrong way. This is the whole shebang, explored in seven steps.

This book contains weekly groups sessions and daily personal studies. Also, in the back of this study is a leader guide with helpful suggestions to use during group time. As you close each group time, encourage students to complete the homework days that follow. Once students have completed this study, they will have learned valuable, biblical tools for finding and keeping lasting friendships.

WHY SHOULD YOU DO A BIBLE STUDY ABOUT FRIENDSHIP?

Because I don't know anyone who doesn't want friends. But I know lots of girls who worry about being unfriended. Or misunderstood. Or hurt or judged or left out or taken for granted by their friends. I'm one of them. So they stop trying. They stop risking. They stop starting over. Because they've stopped believing there'll be a seat saved for them at lunch.

That's what this study is about. It's about not giving up on friendship. Even when we're frustrated by it. Even when we're tired of it, confused by it, or disappointed in it. This study is a chance to make changes.

This is a practical guide to finding and keeping lasting friendships.

This is believing that there really is a seat saved for you at the table. And it's also about becoming the kind of person who will always save a seat for the girls around her. Because, the ultimate friend, Jesus—the friend of the popular and unpopular, of students and teachers, of awkward teens and their minivan driving moms—put it pretty plain and simple. When asked what the greatest commandment was, He said,

> "Love the Lord your God with all your heart, with all your soul, and with all your mind. This is the greatest and most important command. The second is like it: *Love your neighbor as yourself. All the Law and the Prophets depend on these two commands.*" —MATTHEW 22:36-40 (EMPHASIS MINE)

And when pressed to define who exactly this neighbor is that we're commanded to love, He gave a story. And it defines neighbor not as a particular "who," but instead as a "what": as in *what* you should *do*. The parable of the Good Samaritan isn't about *identifying* your neighbor; it's about *being* a neighbor. In essence, it's about being the kind of friend you wish you had.

While we might have defined friendship our whole lives by what others do to us, in the end it's what we do for others that will define us as friends or not. That's how we get friendship to stick. And that's what this study is about. Let's do this together.

—Lisa-Jo

THE
cardinal
rule of
FRIENDSHIP
is you have to
BE WILLING
to go FIRST

#WSYAS

FRIENDSHIP TAKES SHOWING UP

For God loved the world in this way: He gave his one and only Son, so that everyone who believes in him will not perish but have eternal life.

JOHN 3:16

Friendship takes Showing up

Do you think it's difficult to make lasting friendships as girls? Explain.

READ JAMES 3:18.

And the fruit of righteousness is sown in peace by those who cultivate peace.

I particularly like the way The Message paraphrases this verse:

You can develop a healthy, robust community that lives right with God and enjoy its results only if you do the hard work of getting along with each other, treating each other with dignity and honor.

What did James say about our personal responsibility in friendship?

Even from the very beginning, there was a community of three. We were literally built for community—God breathed into our DNA the need for community.

How have you seen this truth in your own life?

Anytime we face a new school year or join a new Bible study group, we're afraid of not fitting in, of not being able to make new friends within a group. We can feel nervous or vulnerable when facing a new group of people because we all bring a history of friendships—both good and bad—with us. But that doesn't mean there is something wrong with us or that we should stop trying.

How can authentic conversation (beyond "I'm fine") be difficult for you or others? Why is it so much easier for us to hide behind simple answers rather than be truthful and vulnerable about our lives?

By allowing others to see us as not simply fine all the time and opening ourselves to vulnerabilities, we develop a trust with those we bring into our lives.

Discuss how we can "give permission" to one another to be "not fine," to enter into a more authentic and personal conversation.

What are some excuses we use to not show up? (For example: "I have too much homework.")

READ ROMANS 12:15 ALOUD. How might excuses be stopping us from living out the message in this verse? How does this affect your ability to build community?

By refusing to be interrupted, we are blocking our friends from honestly sharing with us. None of us are perfect, even though we may want others to think we are. Refusing to hide behind perfect answers and fake smiles will allow our friends to openly share and interrupt our Instagram perfect lives. Jesus was willingly interrupted because He placed people ahead of a set schedule.

Learning to love our friends in the best way is not something we may instinctively know how to do. While you may need to hear words of encouragement, that may not be the best way to be a good friend to others. The way others show love to you is usually evidence of how they best receive love. Think about your friends and how you can love them in the best way. Don't wait for friends to come to you, but show up in intentional ways to initiate and connect.

How can you be an intentional friend who connects in meaningful ways?

Think about a time when you were lonely, even while standing in a crowd. Journal about your experience and consider how it could have been different if someone had taken the opportunity to show up in an intentional way and connect. How can you use your own experience to show up for someone else?

DAY 1

BELIEVE WHAT GOD
SAYS ABOUT FRIENDSHIP

Would you believe that nothing could make the God who gave up His title, His throne, His realm, and His only Son for you ever consider unfriending you? No matter how hangry you are, how tired, frustrated, or unloving.

Because that's where we need to start, at the beginning of the first friendship: God's friendship with the human beings He created. This is the roadmap for all future friendships.

What if I told you that neither social media nor church cliques, friendship breakups nor family disapproval, bad moods nor all your undone homework will ever be able to separate you from the radical, never-giving-up, never-looking-back love of God? A love that proved itself when it took deep breaths in the flesh and blood body of Jesus Christ who literally moved into the neighborhood so that He could be up close and personal friends with you and who has promised that He will never leave you nor forsake you.

Would you believe me?

What is going through your head right now? I know talking about friendship can stir up a lot of feelings and a lot of memories—both good and bad. So, let's unpack some of those. What's the first thing that comes to mind when you think about friendship? Just jot it down without editing yourself. It's okay to be brutally honest.

When I think about friendship, I feel:

finding a person I feel comfortable with and can love with

When I think about friendship, I remember:

good friends I had
bad friends who surprised me

When I think about friendship, I wish:

I don't know about you, but when I think about friendship my stomach can knot up. Sure, I can feel warm and fuzzy about it some days. I have close friends who wrap me in safety and loving acceptance. But when I really think about it, the idea of friendship can spark hundreds of painful memories. Days spent awkwardly trying not to cry on the bus or panic checking my phone in the middle of the night, or trying to act like it's no big deal when I'm not invited to the party everyone was talking about at school.

Friendship is not easy. It's not always fun. It's rarely like the commercials or "squad goals" photos the world would like us to believe. Because nothing hurts as much as the unkind words of a friend. Even the careless words that weren't intended to cut can leave scars.

I've heard too many stories, cried with too many girls, and apologized too many times to think I'm the only one with these bruises on my heart and holes in my story where friends fell through.

I'm guessing you can relate.

I'm guessing there are days you just want to be done with it all. It feels like too much extra work when your plate's already full and you're already juggling a circus of commitments. You don't need one more to-do, especially from a person who wants nothing to do with you. It's so much easier to just chuck it and be done with it all.

But here's the thing—I believe that it is both physically and spiritually impossible to simply wash our hands of other people.

As much as you might try to quit it, friendship is literally woven into your bones. With every breath you take, about 20 breaths per minute, you are entirely dependent on the life breathed into you by a God whose entire existence is a living, breathing friendship of three. He has designed friendship into your DNA, so trying to cut friendship out of your life is like trying to cut out a piece of yourself. It will hurt. It will leave open wounds. I hope I can convince you that it's not worth it—and that it's not healthy for your soul.

> So let's go back to that beginning. Read Genesis 1:1. Who is the very first character we meet in the Bible?

Many scholars believe that the Hebrew word used to name this character in the first verse is *Elohim*. This is significant because *Elohim* is the plural form of that Hebrew word.

In the next few chapters of Genesis, God would refer to Himself in the plural form twice more.

READ GENESIS 1:26a AND GENESIS 3:22a.

What are the two pronouns God used to refer to Himself in these verses?

From the very first sentences of the story of God and the people He created, we are introduced to Him as a holy friendship that we call the Trinity—one God, in three different Persons. Those three parts of God might be as familiar to you as your own name or they might be a brand new idea. Either way, let's read 2 Corinthians 13:13-14 and list each of the three Persons who make up our one God as well as the character trait Paul associated with each of them:

1. The _Grace_ of _Jesus_
2. The _Love_ of _God_
3. The _Fellowship_ of _the holy spirit_

Genesis is the first place we get to overhear God having a conversation with Himself. And this won't be the last time. Throughout Jesus' life, we will get to overhear God the Son having conversations with God the Father, and we will hear God the Son talking about God the Holy Spirit.

One of the most moving times we get to listen in on the friendship between our three-in-one God is the tender moment of Jesus' baptism—where all three Persons of the Trinity are specifically mentioned.

READ MATTHEW 3:13-17. Identify each part of the Trinity and what they each said/did in verses 16-17:

When __Jesus__ was baptized, he went up immediately from the water. The heavens suddenly opened for him, and he saw the __holy spirt__ _____ _____ descending like a __dove__ and coming down on him. And a voice from heaven said: "This is My __beloved Son__, with whom I am well-pleased!"

The profound tenderness and holy joy that rippled through that moment can give you goose bumps! Here is blessing, friendship, benediction, and delight all wrapped up into a single recorded moment in history. This was God publicly celebrating and delighting in the most sacred of relationships—His own.

We have been modeled on and built out of that DNA, made in an image that bears the permanent mark of friendship. We are intended for friendship with God and friendship with each other. But from the very beginning, Satan has tried to burn that image out of us.

Once Satan spewed his first temptation and Adam and Eve doubted God and then disobeyed God, we see the backlash of our broken relationship with God ripping through history. From Adam and Eve, to Cain and Abel, to Noah and his community, to Abraham and Lot, to Saul and David, to Mary and Martha, to the squabbling disciples and down through our Biblical family tree to you and me, Satan is on a campaign to convince us to doubt God and distrust each other.

But our faithful God has been just as determined to keep putting back together the original friendship that got broken. The entire story of Scripture hinges on how Jesus has come to restore our relationships, first with God and second with each other. In the verse that is the heartbeat of God's friendship with us, we read:

> For God loved the world in this way: He gave his one and only Son, so that everyone who believes in him will not perish but have eternal life. —JOHN 3:16

It's the entire reason why Jesus was on earth and available to be baptized. He came to make things right between Himself and us, so that we could live at peace with God as well as with the other human beings God created and placed in our lives.

LET'S READ FROM COLOSSIANS TOGETHER:

He [Jesus] is the beginning,
the firstborn from the dead,
so that He might come to have
first place in everything.
For God was pleased to have
all his fullness dwell in him,
and through him to reconcile
everything to himself
whether things on earth or things in heaven,
by making peace
through his blood, shed on the cross.
　　—COLOSSIANS 1:18b-20 (EMPHASIS MINE)

Everything. Every single broken heart, every twisted family tie, every crushed spirit and wounded relationship, every single thing that has breath to breathe and tears to cry—*everything* is able and intended to be reconciled to God through His Son, Jesus Christ. Such is His wild and wonderful love for us, the creatures created in His image.

And in the final conversation Jesus the Son had with God the Father before He was betrayed and crucified, we get to hear firsthand how passionately Jesus felt about that assignment.

In one of His final prayers before He was arrested, falsely charged, and crucified, some of Jesus' very last words to His Father were about His friends—the people entrusted to Him. What did He say about them?

GO AND READ JOHN 17:6-19.

Jesus could tell His Father in no uncertain terms, that as far as it was possible for Him, He had kept the faith and the friendship of every one of the friends entrusted to Him. Even Judas had been included right up until the moment He chose to quit Jesus, not the other way around.

Highlight verse 12 in your Bible.

Now put your own name into the verse:

"While I was with _Shelby_____, I was protecting [her] by your name that you have given me. I guarded _Shelby____ ..." (John 17:12).

When you hear the word *protected,* what does it bring to mind? List a few words you associate with the idea of being "protected."

When you hear the word *guarded,* what does it bring to mind? List a few words you associate with the idea of being "guarded."

Both words are significant cornerstones of what it means to be God's friend. The commentaries spend a lot of time unpacking the power of these words. *Protection* gives us the image of a shepherd tenderly caring for and feeding his flock, while *guarding* implies the kind of actions that would bravely protect you from all kinds of wild beasts determined to rip your life to shreds.[1]

Taking the image even further, the Greek word Jesus used when He talked about guarding His disciples meant the kind of protection you'd get "behind the walls of a fortress."[2] Those are the very walls Jesus wraps around you—to guard and protect you by His Holy Spirit. You are so dear to Him. He is the friend who gave up His very life to protect you. He is the friend who lived up to His own definition of love and friendship.

WRITE THE DEFINITION FROM JOHN 15:13.

"No one has greater love than this: _____."

He is the friend who is with you, protecting you, and guarding you, even with His own life.

Now think of the people in your life. Picture the faces of your friends—even the ones who have frustrated, irritated, or hurt you. Can you put them into this sentence?

"While I was with _____, I was protecting [her] by your name that you have given me. I guarded _____ ..." (John 17:12).

Can you do that? Are you willing to be a safe place for them—a friend who will offer the walls of protection and compassion like a fortress around them?

That's what this study is about: believing that we are safely guarded by Jesus' friendship and being willing to put our friends—the people trusted to us—into that sentence. We're called to become guards around their lives with real friendship—friendship that doesn't hold back, that always believes the best because we're convinced that is how serious God is about His friendship with us.

But until we have that truth cemented into the foundation of our identity, we will not be able to give that kind of friendship to other people. For that kind of friendship to be possible, you need to believe it first for yourself. So as we get started on this journey together, please take this truth and deposit it—use super glue if necessary—into the very core of who you are: Jesus guarded His friends—that includes you and me—with His very life.

Friendship Challenge

Write out this verse and stick it on your mirror, in your locker, or set it as the lock screen on your phone so that we can begin to superglue its truth to our souls. Be sure to write your own name, as well as the name of at least one friend, into the blanks:

"While I was with _____, I was protecting [her] by your name that you have given me. I guarded _____ ..." (John 17:12).

BE WILLING TO
BE INTERRUPTED

If you ask people how they're doing these days you'll likely hear one of two responses: either "I'm fine" or "I'm so busy." We live in a world where politeness overrides honesty and productivity overrides rest. So the last thing anyone expects to hear in response to the question, "How are you?" is the truth. Because some days that might sound like: I'm crazy excited about making the volleyball team, I'm so thankful for my amazing friends, or I'm enjoying a quiet afternoon napping or reading a book.

But, there are other answers that are harder to share, so we tend to shove them deep down inside of us where they can't slip out and shock anyone: *I'm exhausted, I'm depressed, I don't think I can stand my little sister, I'm overwhelmed, I'm lonely, I'm still grieving, I'm maxed out,* or *I'm about to lose my mind.* It feels awkward to interrupt someone else's day by shoving onto them the unexpected baggage of how we're *actually* doing. It feels like an inconvenience. An interruption. And an imposition on their time.

So we get really good at faking fine and keeping our baggage tucked neatly away so that it doesn't spill over into the lives and afternoons of the people around us. That would be embarrassing and awkward. What happens when you tell someone how you're really doing and they don't have time for it?

If there's one thing that defined Jesus' time on earth—it was His willingness to be interrupted. And not just that there were constant interruptions (and good grief were there a ridiculous amount of those!). What's so striking is how instead of being annoyed by interruptions, He *welcomed* them.

Let's compare how we feel/act about interruptions to how Jesus responded to being interrupted.

First, make a list of how *you* think *other people* will react if you interrupt their day to tell them how you're *really* doing and ask for help instead of just giving the default answer: "I'm fine." (I've filled in the first two to get you started.)

I'm worried if I tell people how I'm really doing they will feel:

Awkward

Embarrassed

Now, let's make a list of how you might react if someone interrupted *your* day to tell you how they're really doing and to ask for help.

If someone else shared how she was really doing, instead of just saying she was "fine," I'd feel:

Surprised

Nervous

Now, let's spend some time with Jesus to see how His days and His interruptions looked. If we trace several days in His life as chronicled by His disciples, Matthew and Mark, this is what we find:

VERSES	WHERE WAS JESUS GOING?	WHO INTERRUPTED HIM?	WHAT DID THEY WANT?	WHAT DID JESUS DO?
Matthew 8:5-13	To the city of Capernaum	Soider	him to heal his servant	healed him with words from a far
Matthew 8:14-15	To Peter's house			
Matthew 8:18,23-27	To the other side of the Sea of Galilee	his disiples	The storm to end	end the storm
Matthew 8:28-34	To the region of the Gadarenes			
Matthew 9:1-8	Back across the sea to His own town (Capernaum)	paralyzed man	to heal him	told the man to walk and he did
Matthew 9:18-19,23-26	To teach His disciples			
Matthew 9:20-22	To Jairus' house			
Matthew 9:27-30	He went "on from there" (from Jairus' house) to another house	two blind men	to see	he gave them sight with hands
Mark 10:46-52	Leaving Jericho	blind man	to see	
Matthew 19:13-15	To teach His disciples	children	To spend time with them	he prayed for them, and taked to them

Jesus stopped *every single time*. He allowed Himself to be interrupted, detoured, and inconvenienced. It was never the perfect time and never in a perfect setting. This is eye-opening for me—the woman who has been known to shove dirty dishes into the microwave and/or hide in the bedroom when unexpected visitors stop by., because by Sunday afternoon our house often looks like a three ring circus passed through. Every surface is covered in teetering stacks of school books or papers, and shoes, backpacks, socks, (don't ask me why) gym shorts, and pencils flung every which way around the front door and in a chaotic trail down the hall.

If I'm being honest, I even freak out about the planned visits. I admit I like the perfectly planned setting, food, and a visit that has a set start and end time. But hanging out doesn't always happen in a perfectly planned way. Sometimes, people will come over before your homework is finished or before you've had a chance to clean your room.

Girls, I used to allow my imperfect house—the way you'd find it on a Sunday afternoon—keep me from inviting people over.

But the thing is, being willing to be interrupted isn't about the state of our houses or our rooms. It's about the state of our hearts. Friends aren't looking for perfection; they're looking for connection. One of the ways our world of the fast and furious Internet hurts us is that our schedules and attention spans often don't have enough time to give each other uninterrupted hours of conversation. But we will starve on a diet of conversations limited to 140 character tweets, text messages, or Facebook status updates. We need soul food conversations. The kind that don't cut you off because they have somewhere else to be. The kind that stick with you.

I learned this the hard way through a selfish, split-second moment when I wasn't willing to make time for a friend—when I wasn't willing to be interrupted, when I wasn't willing to stick around. I would take it back if I could, but I can't because my friend passed away a couple weeks after the night I avoided her.

I remember it with a knot in my stomach. It was a night when I was tired after a late church event. All I wanted was to wrangle everyone back into the minivan, go home, and go to bed. I wanted my shoes off, my hair down, and my comfy pants on. As I was crossing through the church hall, I kept my eyes down so that I wouldn't have to stumble into conversation with anyone.

I wove my way through the chairs trying to get to my kids and spotted one of my Tuesday night Bible study girls with her back to me and her hand on her cane. Without even giving it a second thought, I backtracked around her so I wouldn't have to pause to talk—to give up a second of my stupid, selfish time to a friend who lived by herself in a small room with her cats and her passion for beautiful, colorful necklaces, and who came out every Tuesday night because she was so desperate for company.

Just a few weeks later she had a stroke that she never recovered from. She died before there was a chance for any more nights together. It was a small invisible moment that she didn't even know I stole from her, but I did steal it. And it was the last time I saw her alive. I only saw her back because my tired, selfish heart avoided a friend when it should have given the gift of its own time and presence. I know better. And I have to live with that memory. Time is a gift that doesn't even belong to me, but was gifted by God, who spoke hours and minutes into being the moment He set the sun and the moon in the sky.

I stood at her memorial service, and I got to see the generous way she spent her life. I got to hear from person after person about how she'd poured herself into each one of them. We laughed, cried, and sang our hearts out in memory of a woman who was quirky and beloved, and I loved her too. She wasn't perfect—and she knew I wasn't either—but now I get to carry her in my heart where she reminds me that giving people our time is an act of radical generosity. It's counter cultural to refuse to say those three words we say without even thinking: "I'm too busy." I don't want "too busy." I want to be available. I want to be willing to be interrupted. Period.

Dietrich Bonhoeffer describes it like this in his book, *Life Together:*

> We must be ready to allow ourselves to be interrupted by God. God will be constantly crossing our paths and canceling our plans by sending us people with claims and petitions. We may pass them by, preoccupied with our more important tasks. ... It is a strange fact that Christians and even ministers frequently consider their work so important and urgent that they will allow nothing to disturb them. They think they are doing God a service in this, but actually they are disdaining God's "crooked yet straight path."[3]

Friendship Challenge

So, let's get real honest together. Write down the names of specific people who felt like an interruption to your week. Let's flip that on its head and consider what God might actually be asking us to say to them or do with them. Maybe it's as simple as listening, taking a walk, doing a project, or sharing a movie night. Now, pray over those girls, and ask God what He'd like you to do for them this week.

- teachers/homework
- family members
- rude people
- daily tasks
- mr R/ms boikyon

• Some company members

DAY 3

CRY AND
CELEBRATE TOGETHER

So far, I'm hoping we've learned at least two things about friendship together: One, God is your forever friend; Two, friendship welcomes interruptions. And along the way there really isn't room for worrying what your friends will think about the current state of your life, because true friends are more interested in the state of your heart than the state of your room. I love how The Message describes the incarnation—that sacred moment when God wrapped Himself up in human skin, feelings, body, and soul. John 1:14 says: "The Word became flesh and blood and moved into the neighborhood" (MSG). Jesus closed the gap between God and us by pulling up a chair alongside us in our daily lives so that we could know Him as He made Himself known to us.

We are invited to do the same thing Jesus did: give the gift of our presence. We are called to be willing to experience life with the community around us, showing up and doing one of two things.

READ ROMANS 12:15 and write down what they are:

" *rejoice* with those who *rejoice* ; *weep* with those who *weep* ."

In other words, showing up for our friends can look as simple as doing the ugly cry with them or joining their celebrations with whooping and hollering and confetti. It sounds simple, but it takes discipline. It takes intentionality. And more often than we admit, it takes courage.

Jesus' example is so radical because He lived it. He lived out the entire range of human emotions—from weddings to funerals. He rejoiced and He wept in public, and we have it recorded in Scripture. Two of what might be His most well-known miracles took place in these settings—the joy of a wedding and the despair of a death.

Read both stories and describe in your own words what the atmosphere might have been like at each event:

John 2:1-11: **wedding, celebrating, best for last, shame**

John 11:17-36:

Sad, weeping

According to John 11:3, how did Jesus feel about Lazarus? How did Lazarus' sisters describe his relationship with Jesus?

Jesus loved Lazarus

The emotional energy at both events was off the charts—delight and despair, passion and gut-wrenching grief, hope, and doubt. And Jesus willingly stepped into both environments and into the deep well of human emotions. I don't know about you, but sometimes I can be intimidated by the emotional highs and lows of my friends. It can be tough to know the right words to say in the midst of their grief or how to balance their celebration with my own insecurities. Those are the nitty-gritty details behind the scenes of Romans 12:15, which is why I love getting a glimpse at the details surrounding Jesus' interactions with His friends in both their highs and their lows.

Bible commentaries allow us to paint a vivid picture of what those moments meant to the people living them. Behind the scenes of the story of the wedding in Cana we learn that:

> A wedding is always a gala occasion, and in a village like Cana it would be a community celebration. "Refreshments" were provided for all guests. ... To fail in providing adequately for the guests would involve social disgrace. In the closely knit communities of Jesus' day, such an error would never be forgotten and would haunt the newly married couple all their lives. The situation prompted Mary's urgency when she informed Jesus of the emergency.[4]

Dancing, love, laughter, and passion. Seven days of joy, food, family, and of telling stories and catching up on life and celebrating—and the vital importance of being able to provide generously for all your guests. And there was Jesus, right at the heart of it.

And a death? The desperate despair of loss. In the shortest verse in recorded Scripture we know that "Jesus wept" (John 11:35). Commentaries paint for us the nuances so that we can see and experience the picture more vividly:

> The third word, … (edakrusen, "wept"), means to shed tears quietly. It may be contrasted with the loud and ostentatious weeping…of the hired mourners (v. 33), which was artificial. … Jesus' sorrow impressed the onlookers with the depth of his concern.[5]

Are we brave enough to follow His example and open our hearts up to the raw emotions of our friends?

Describe your honest reaction to someone else's scary sorrow.

My Granda and uncle at a funeral.

Describe your honest reaction to someone else's overpowering joy.

I was surprised because I had never seen that.

Recently, over hamburgers and corn on the cob, our pastor's wife told me how she's spent the last four years walking with a friend through the long, slow, terrible valley of grief. I was sort of stunned. Four years! Who has the guts to go that kind of distance? Who has it in them to commit to a friend through the terrible roller coaster of grief for that long? It's rare. It's holy. It's heroic. It's a gift.

> After my mom died, I had friends quit on me because my grief was too heavy to carry. I don't blame them. There were many days I wished I could quit it myself. Grief is exhausting, and if you have the choice, it's a luxury to choose to avoid it. But on an ordinary Monday afternoon, there was this woman of faith telling me how she knew from the get-go that she was going to commit to the whole journey through grief with her friend.

Because like all difficult and painful things, the only way through is through. And if you have a friend willing to walk that dark road with you, then you might have a decent chance of making it out on the other side. But even with a friend by your side, it will be challenging to find the bits and pieces of yourself to put them back together again in a pattern you can recognize in the mirror.

The strange thing about joy is that it can have the same effect—sometimes it's too exhausting for our friends to embrace. Sometimes our joy pricks at the parts of their own lives where they're dissatisfied. Sometimes our joy highlights their hurts or losses. There are days when someone else's joy feels more like a threat than a celebration. The crazy underbelly of joy taints when it should encourage, threatens when it should inspire, diminishes when it should enlarge.

Ask any girl struggling with insecurity how she feels when her friends all receive perfect promposals. Ask any motherless daughter how Mother's Day feels or any athlete how it feels to be cut from the team. You know what I'm talking about, right?

When was the last time you were so sad you felt like what your soul was experiencing was bigger than your body could contain? When was the last time your soul wept?

Kitty died

When was the last time you were so filled with delight and the desire to share your news and celebrate with someone that you couldn't possibly hold it all in? When was the last time your soul rejoiced?

Lock-IN

The cool thing about Jesus is that through all of those experiences, He is in the business of making all things new. Write out Revelation 21:5 (the first part of the verse):

God, in His infinite wisdom and His inability to be limited by sin, is constantly transforming our lives and our faith. Literally. In the stories we studied today, Jesus used both sets of experiences to transform. To make something new. To transform water into something much more special. To transform death into life. Both moments are evidence of Jesus' transformative nature. In His kingdom nothing is wasted; no grief or joy is left to stand alone. Both are arrows pointing us back to the God who is constantly transforming us more and more into His own image.

If we will bravely enter into the joy and sorrow of our friends it will transform both of us because it will always point us back to Christ. Listen to how *The Expositor's Bible Commentary* describes the transformative nature of Jesus' first miracle—the one that worked a change way beyond what happened to the water:

The purpose of Jesus' first miracle after entering Galilee is not stated. ... The nature of the miracle is very plain. Jesus had come to bring about conversion: water to wine, sinners to saints. And this latter miracle of transformation occurred in almost complete obscurity. Few know when or how it happened, but they know that it did happen.

The effect of this miracle is noteworthy. It marked the beginning of a ministry accompanied by supernatural power; and it proved so convincing to the new disciples that they "put their faith in him." The deed helped confirm the conclusion they had drawn from their previous interviews with him: Jesus must be the Messiah.[6]

At a wedding, in a totally unexpected way, Jesus began His ministry of transformation— of making all things new—starting with the people around Him. The delightful quality of the miracle He performed on the water wasn't about the pleasure it brought to the guests. It was about the change He was offering to bring about in their lives.

This is the same story we see unfold outside a tomb in Bethany:

Why should he be glad that he was not present to save Lazarus from death, or to comfort the sisters, and why should Lazarus's death bring any benefit to the disciples? Jesus considered this an opportunity for a supreme demonstration of power that would certify the Father's accreditation of him as the Son and confirm the faith of the sisters and the disciples. He was certain of the outcome.[7]

To make ourselves vulnerable to experience the grief and the joy of our friends is to make ourselves available to being changed—transformed—by the Christ who is always present on both journeys. When we let our insecurities or awkwardness stop us from fully entering into the experiences of the people around us, we limit the transformative impact the Holy Spirit can have on our lives. Because while we might not know how to put those experiences into words, He does. He's the friend available to process all of it with us.

Write out Romans 8:26.

That second half of the verse is translated in a variety of ways—all of them sweet with the tender intimacy of how closely God is willing to walk with us as we try to make sense of our sorrows and joys and the sorrows and joys of the people around us:

CSB: The Spirit himself intercedes for us with *unspoken groanings.*

NIV: The Spirit Himself intercedes for us through *wordless groans.*

NLT: The Holy Spirit prays for us with *groanings that cannot be expressed in words.*

ESV: The Spirit himself intercedes for us with *groanings too deep for words.*

MSG: He does our praying in and for us, *making prayer out of our wordless sighs, our aching groans.*

—ROMANS 8:26

In every translation we see the raw ability of the Holy Spirit to express even the things we can't manage to put into words ourselves. He is our constant, trustworthy companion as we try to make sense of our experiences and participate in the journeys of the people we love. I don't want to miss that chance. I don't want my own self-consciousness, selfishness, or tiredness to distract me from participating in the life-changing work of God in me and in the people around me.

But I know I have failed, and I will fail again, and so I'm desperate to learn from Jesus' closest friends who stand as a cautionary tale for what not to do when someone we love is desperate for support.

READ MATTHEW 26:36-45, when Jesus' closest friends missed the chance to help Him carry the heavy load of His worry and His grief.

List the emotions Jesus experienced based on what He told His disciples.

Savanna
Sofia
Carter

What distracted the disciples from fully entering into what Jesus went through?

I've always thought the worst betrayal of the night was Peter's denial of Jesus, but the more I studied this passage, the more terrible this moment grew in my mind. In the moment when Peter denied Jesus we don't know if there was anything he could have actually said or done to bring comfort to Jesus, his dearest friend.

But in the garden, in the dark of night, Jesus spelled out exactly what His friends could do to encourage and comfort Him. And they failed Him 100 percent.

Jesus took with Him three disciples into this intimate moment of grief and suffering. What three things did He ask them to do?

The sense of betrayal He must have felt at returning to find them fast asleep, not once, not twice, but three times (interestingly the same number of times Peter would deny Him verbally later that night) probably cut Him deep before He even encountered Judas and the soldiers in the garden.

I'm desperate not to disappoint my Jesus. I'm desperate for His help in keeping watch with Him. I don't want to miss Him. I want to be awake with Him and for Him. But *how,* you might ask. Well, we know that Jesus shows up in the faces, the stories, and the voices, and in the joys and sorrows of the people we encounter on what feels like totally ordinary Mondays, Tuesdays, or Sundays. He shows up in the lives of our tough teachers, our difficult family members, and our struggling friends.

Just one chapter earlier in Matthew 25:40, what had Jesus taught?

It's right there in black and white. If you want to comfort Jesus in His most suffocating sorrows or celebrate with Him in His most tremendous triumphs, you have to start with the people around you—the people Jesus has entrusted to you, the young men and women who bear His image.

Friendship Challenge

Let's start right here, right now. Make a list of the girls in your life who could use your company this week—whether they're walking a journey of joy or sorrow, excitement or despair. After you write their names, make the time to connect with them. And wait and see how you're transformed by meeting Jesus in the lives of the people around you.

It doesn't take much. And sure, sometimes the showing up can make us feel awkward. It might make us feel embarrassed—but only for the few minutes it takes us to stop thinking about ourselves. As soon as we're able to look past ourselves and focus on our friends, the sooner we're able to forget about saying the right thing and simply start saying the next thing.

You might be surprised how helpful that is to keep in mind. Just say the next thing—*pepperoni or cheese? Coffee or tea? I picked up an extra coloring book at the store. Here, I brought this for you. Sit next to me today at lunch. Do you need to borrow a pen or paper? I made cookies. You can eat them while we watch a movie together.* Just keep showing up and saying the next thing and that kind of friendship will wrap itself around our friends' sorrows or joys simply by our willingness to be present.

IF it
is real,
FRIENDSHIP
is usually
untidy

#WSYAS

FRIENDSHIP TAKES VULNERABILITY

Jesus said to her, "I am the resurrection and the life. The one who believes in me, even if he dies, will live."

JOHN 11:25

FriENDship takes VULNERABILITY

When you hear the word *vulnerability*, what memories of friendship come to mind? Share both the good and the bad.

Savanna and Kate

Why do you think vulnerability can feel so awkward?

you don't know how you ever trusted that person

When we find ourselves in these moments requiring honesty and sharing our feelings, it can be scary to take that first step. Many of us would rather hide our feelings and pretend to be perfect than allow others to see our imperfections or fears or ugly cry face. But this can be a shield against forming true friendships.

How does self-sufficiency keep us from being vulnerable with others? What are you hiding from others?

Who is the girl you can share your fears and imperfections with? The girl who can be trusted with your secrets and who you never fear will judge you harshly or gossip about you after? Share an experience where the Lord has provided the right person for a season of your life. Maybe it's even your current best friend.

How have hurts in your past kept you from finding community and being vulnerable with other girls in the present?

It's shocking to realize that you can be hurt by people in church, but it's important to remember that we can also hurt people.

How have hurts within your church group affected your perspective of friendship? What are you learning in this Bible study that could help you overcome this perspective?

In the face of past hurts, it is even more difficult to move past those bad memories and be vulnerable again. But if we stay closed to the idea of new friendships, we could miss the opportunity to meet our new best friend. Think about it this way: Maybe you don't know her well right now, but that new girl in your English class could become your closest friend by graduation.

How has God surprised you through the friendships in your own life?

Vulnerability is such a powerful tool toward healing. We are all broken, and we can use those broken pieces to start healing.

How have you seen evidence of this in your life?

READ JOHN 11:21,32-33.

Mary and Martha were grieving and were not afraid to meet Jesus with their hurt and vulnerable selves. Jesus allowed them to feel that pain and entered their sadness with them. He was also the answer to their hurting. And He is the answer to your hurting.

What if you approached your relationship with Jesus like Mary and Martha—in a real and truthful way? Instead of coming to Jesus in your Sunday best, come to Jesus as your vulnerable self and your truthful self.

How could this change the way you approach relationships—especially in your church groups, Bible study groups, or group of friends?

You don't have to wait until your life is Instagram perfect to come to Jesus. He is the safest place for you to share your deepest hurts and vulnerabilities. David wrote many Psalms speaking directly to the Lord and was honest and broken and never hid his pain from the Lord.

READ PSALM 10 AND PSALM 143.

Then journal your own hurts and pain with open-handed and open-hearted vulnerability.

· I want a better dance lift than Carter. ☹

- I am scared to see the future and what it holds
- I see him in little things but not big that can be hard because once I get faith from something small in my day I easily get let down when I remember the big things going on like dance arts and grades

FRIENDSHIP TAKES VULNERABILITY 35

DAY 1

GET HONEST WITH GOD

Friendship that requires us to open our front doors just the way we are and stop playing "fine" in front of our friends—that makes us make time and won't let us make small talk—can land you feeling emotionally exposed and desperately vulnerable. Like you're standing on your best friend's front doorstep in your pajamas with bed head and ugly cry face left over from the night before, and you're wondering if she's going to open the door. If she's going to be comfortable with this raw version of you. If she's going to invite you in or if she's going to make excuses to move you on out— especially if you didn't text first to let her know you were coming over.

There's this terrifying moment between heartbeats when you don't know what she's going to say or how she's going to react. You're just standing there with all your raw honesty waiting for her to take her turn and respond. Waiting for her to stretch out an arm and wrap you up in a hug or for the frown to appear on her face as she tries to make sense of this version of you, this version that clearly makes her uncomfortable.

In or out. What will it be? As your heart beats and waits and hopes and holds its breath.

Can you trust a friend with all your vulnerability or should you have stopped to grab a brush and some concealer before showing up? Should you have stopped first to get it together and cover up the tears?

Of course the temptation to cover up isn't just about how we look and whether we've cried off our make up or not. It's about taking the risk to show up with our unairbrushed stories of bullying or loss or dating or depression. It's whether we can trust our friends to let us tell them how desperate we are to find ways to cope after the heartache of our first breakup. It's wondering if they will still look at us the same when they hear how angry we sometimes feel toward our siblings, our parents, our God. Will they still accept us if we crack into an awkward fit of weeping at the end of the sofa when we learn just one more friend has a new boyfriend and we're still single?

Where can we take all these vulnerable feelings if we can't take them to our friends? Can we come out of hiding and let ourselves be really seen? Can we just stand there in the middle of our lives and let our friends read right up to where we are and trust them with what comes next, even when we have no idea what that might be?

The thing is, trusting our friends is a reflection of how much we are willing to trust the God who created them. Until we can trust God with our vulnerability, it will be impossible to trust other people. Do you? Do you trust God to be a friend who won't let you down, especially if you feel like God *has* let you down.

Can you trust God with your honest feelings? Can you trust Him with your whole vulnerable heart? With your disappointments? Go ahead, tell it like it is.

When have you felt like God has let you down?

It's such an awkward question, isn't it? But it's an honest one. If we can't bring our honest questions and fears that God will (or has) let us down to God Himself, the Author of all our relationships, then who can we ask? And here's the thing, we wouldn't be the first to ask that question. We wouldn't be the first accusing God of letting us down. Mary and Martha already went there.

Those sisters were so comfortable in their friendship with Jesus, so sure of His love and acceptance, that they comfortably accused Him of letting their brother, Lazarus, die when they believed Jesus could have healed him.

That's huge. That's a *wow* kind of accusation. That's nuclear level friendship disappointment. But instead of stewing silently about it, Mary and Martha brought every ounce of their crushing hurt and sadness to Jesus Himself. They absolutely trusted He was the right place to go with that kind of disappointment. Their grief was raw and naked, and they didn't try to hide any of it from Him.

And Jesus?

He took it. He leaned in. He listened. He got it. And He stepped right into the chasm of their own terrible grief until it became His own. And more than that—He responded in uniquely individual ways to each of the sisters. These women so much like each of us—straight-spoken, bold Martha, the doer, and contemplative Mary, the listener.

READ JOHN 11:20.

Describe how each sister responded to hearing that Jesus had finally arrived in their town days after their beloved brother had died.

What did Martha do?	What did Mary do?
martha went to him	mary stayed at home

Martha was a woman of action and that's where Jesus met her grief. She demanded action and He assured her action was coming.

> Then Martha said to Jesus, "Lord, if you had been here, my brother wouldn't have died. Yet even now I know that whatever you ask from God, God will give you." —JOHN 11:21-22

I love how Martha was not-so-subtly prodding Jesus to *do* something already.

In verse 23 what action did Jesus assure her would come?

He said that their brother would rise again.

And sweet, determined Martha, I can just imagine her heart sinking heavy into her chest as she said to her dear friend Jesus, "I know that he will rise again in the resurrection at the last day" (v. 24). That feels so far off, doesn't it? "The last day" is a long and terrible time to wait to be reunited. Any of us who've lost people know how terrible that kind of wait can feel.

But Jesus had an answer for Martha's action-hungry heart. Standing before her, the friend she was afraid might have disappointed her trust, proved Himself deeply faithful. He looked into her eyes that must have been bloodshot from crying and said to her with what I imagine must have been unspeakable tenderness combined with unshakable assurance:

> "*I am* the resurrection and the life. The one who believes in me, even if he dies, will live." —JOHN 11:25, (EMPHASIS MINE)

I mean! There He was, standing before her, the living answer to her crushing disappointment and desperate hunger for action. *He* is "the resurrection and the life." This friend Himself carries the answer within His holy, God-breathed DNA. He was God's response to her desperate desire for action in the face of death. Life runs in His veins and He offered it to Martha and He offers it to you and me.

> Jesus asks us the same question He asked Martha in verse 26:
> "Do __Belive__ this?"
>   ^
>   you

Do we? Can we? Dare we take Him at His word?

Martha did. And being the wonderful woman of action that she was, she ran back to her sister Mary and told her,

> "The Teacher is here and is calling for you." —JOHN 11:28

Then it was Mary's turn to take her disappointed friendship to her friend, Jesus. To keep on being vulnerable even in the face of bruised trust.

> The same adverb was used twice to describe how Mary went to Jesus (vv. 29,31). What was it?

She didn't hesitate to go to Jesus. She didn't hide or sulk—she went at once to the friend who could make sense of what happened to them. It had been four days since her brother died and her exhausted tears were still brimming over as she fell at Jesus' feet and repeated what her sister had already said,

> "Lord, if you had been here, my brother would not have died!"
> —JOHN 11:32

That exclamation mark at the end of the sentence cuts deep when I read it. It's the point of the knife digging into my heart, and I can imagine it felt the same to Jesus.

Look at His reaction to Mary. No calm or rational conversation about what comes next. In response to this sister and her outpouring of emotion, we see Jesus mirror her grief with His own.

> When Jesus saw her crying, and the Jews who had come with her crying, he was deeply moved in his spirit and troubled. —JOHN 11:33

Other versions translate the word "crying" as "weeping" (NIV). And it's not a quiet or polite kind of crying. No, it's the kind of loud, awkward, terrible, almost inhuman sound of grief that can terrify and embarrass listeners. The *NIV Study Bible* tells us, "Both times the word denotes a loud expression of grief, i.e., 'wailing.'"[1] And then overcome by emotion, Jesus Himself burst into tears in what might be the most vulnerable verse in Scripture: "Jesus wept" (v. 35).

Ours is a God we can vent to, ours is a God who will cry with us, but most crucial—ours is a God who will raise our deepest hurts from the dead because He is just as angry as we are at what sin steals from us. The Greek word used in John 11:33 for "angry" most likely means that Jesus was angry "over sin and death which could cause such agony."[2] And then our Jesus, our God who understands our human emotions of grief and disappointment from the inside out—from inside the very skin of humanity—proves Himself faithful and powerful enough to raise back to life what was once dead. Jesus raised Lazarus, who had been dead for days, by name—just like He will raise you and me, just like He calls us by name. What is required from us in order to see that glory of God in action?

> Jesus said to her, "Didn't I tell you that if you believed you would see the glory of God?"—JOHN 11:40

We have to *believe* in order for Him to raise us and our dead and disappointed hearts from the tomb. Can we do it? Can we bring our broken hearts to Him and trust in Him, believe in Him so that we will hear His voice call us by name and raise back to life everything we thought had died in us and in our friendships? Dare we be that vulnerable with our God, our friend, and our Father? Maybe the better question is, how do we dare *not?*

Friendship Challenge

If vulnerability starts with Jesus, what do you need to tell Him today? What have you been holding back? Can you trust Him to mourn it with you and then to raise it back up from the dead?

> On one side of a note card or piece of paper, fill in this sentence as honestly as possible:
>
> *Lord, if you had been here my* Bucky/Senior c./Lilly *wouldn't have died.* (And remember, it doesn't have to be a person—it could be a dream, a hope, a project, or a relationship. Be specific.)

Let Him weep with you; He's just as angry as you are about that terrible loss.

Now, let's trust Him to raise it from the dead.

> On the other side of the card write down and then pray this prayer with Jesus: "Father, I thank you that you heard me. I know that you always hear me" (John 11:41b-42a). Then write this sentence: *I believe I will see the glory of God.*

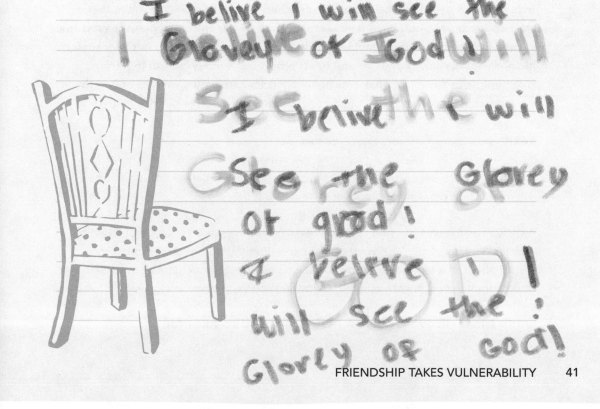

I believe I will see the
I Gloreye of God will
SI believe will
see the glorey
or god!
I believe I
will see the:
Glorey of God!

DAY 2

STOP TRYING TO BE IMPRESSIVE
AND START BEING YOU

Once you believe that God loves you just the way you are, you can start to open your door and your life to let other people into the messy parts. This is the way we help our friends feel at home in our houses as well as in our lives. Then even our disappointments become appointments with the God who raises all broken things from the dead. Can we become so secure in our vulnerability with Jesus that it spills over into trusting others with that same kind of vulnerability? Will we open our doors and our lives to the people around us who might also disappoint us? Let me rephrase that, to the people around us who will definitely disappoint us at some point?

Maybe we're worried that if we let people see us or know us (how we really are) then we'll lose their admiration or respect. Worse yet, maybe we're afraid they'll unfollow us. Maybe that's why we're so attached to the picture of ourselves that we've constructed. After all, we've been groomed by our culture to present a flawless version of ourselves to the people around us. We edit our rooms and our Facebook pictures, our Instagram updates and filters reflect our Sunday best so that they communicate a version of ourselves that reflects the person we want to be. Maybe, if we're honest, these things don't reflect the version of ourselves that we actually are.

So let's start there. Complete this sentence:

I want people to think that I am _____ because I'm afraid they won't like me if they discover I am actually _____.

It's OK. We all have a version of ourselves we'd prefer instead of our actual reality. This is why I love Paul. The apostle with exceedingly grand qualifications, who wasn't afraid to wave them around on the one hand but on the other hand was utterly unimpressed by his own bio. Come and see for yourself.

GO TO PHILIPPIANS 3:3-6 AND READ PAUL'S RÉSUMÉ.

Focus on verses 5 and 6, and list Paul's seven most impressive résumé qualifications under *Paul's Credentials*. (We'll fill in *Paul's Reality* later.)

	PAUL'S CREDENTIALS	PAUL'S REALITY
1.		
2.		
3.		
4.		
5.		
6.		
7.		

Paul's life was the picture perfect appearance of godliness, holiness, and piety. It was the pinnacle of accomplishment in his time and culture. But Paul was totally unimpressed by his own credentials, because he had a ringside seat to the state of his own heart.

READ 1 TIMOTHY 1:15.

How did Paul describe himself in this verse?

Paul, never one to mince words, says he considers all his so-called accomplishments, "garbage, that I may gain Christ and be found in him, not having a righteousness of my own that comes from the law, but that which is through faith in Christ" (Phil. 3:8-9, NIV).

Paul painted a gripping picture for us of the truth that was first spoken to the prophet Samuel before he anointed a young, unheard of shepherd boy named David the future king of Israel. When none of the seven strapping sons that were presented to Samuel were identified by God's Spirit as the future king, Samuel was stumped. And I love God's response in the language from the New King James translation:

But the LORD said to Samuel, "Do not look at his appearance or at his physical stature, because I have refused him. *For the LORD does not see as man sees; for man looks at the outward appearance, but the LORD looks at the heart.*" —1 SAMUEL 16:7 (NKJV; EMPHASIS MINE)

We can crop and highlight and filter ourselves within an inch of our lives, but the Holy Spirit sees through the lies with all knowing eyes that penetrate into the core of our hearts. There is no hiding, no filtering, no editing the truth of who we are from God. Paul knew this. And when it comes to stripping himself down to his bare bones under the gaze of the church in Corinth who have become star struck by the so-called "super-apostles" of the day, Paul turned fame on its head when his only claims to it were a long list of his failures.

Go back to the chart we started about Paul. Now, fill in the right column with all the disasters and painful losses listed in 2 Corinthians 11:24-33 that characterized Paul's actual ministry. There are a lot of them aren't there?

Rather than camouflaging his shame, his abuse, his crushing torture, Paul leaned into this weakness as the only safe place because:

"[God's] power is perfected in weakness." Therefore, I will most gladly boast all the more about my weaknesses, so that Christ's power may reside in me. So I take pleasure in weaknesses, insults, hardships, persecutions, and in difficulties, for the sake of Christ. For when I am weak, then I am strong."
—2 CORINTHIANS 12:9b-10

We live in a culture that's uncomfortable with weakness—one that would prefer to dress up even our weaknesses as strengths. But as Pastor Tim Keller wrote,

Like Paul, we can say, "I don't care what you think. I don't even care what I think. I only care about what the Lord thinks."[3]

Can we say that? Are we willing to lean into that kind of self-forgetfulness? Because surely that's the only way to freedom. The only way to cut through the sticky web of personal promotion that spans the corridors of our lives, our TVs, our smartphones, and our tired minds.

I believe it's a choice with life and death consequences, because women are starving for more than status updates and 140 character connections. It's up to you and me to let them in so that they can discover that they're not alone in their doubts, their fears, and their failures. So they can trust that we will be friends who are the same versions of ourselves, whether online or over a stack of homework due tomorrow.

People will feel the most at home with you if you're willing to let them see you at your most real. Can we rethink the idea of our "Sunday best" together? What if our Sunday Best really is our most vulnerable self? After all, those are the people invited to come to Jesus:

> "Come to me, all of you who are weary and burdened, and I will give you rest." —MATTHEW 11:28

> "Come, everyone who is thirsty, come to the water; and you without silver, come, buy, and eat! Come, buy wine and milk without silver and without cost!" —ISAIAH 55:1

It's the parched, those with chapped lips and souls, the starving who can't hide their hunger who are invited to come—just as they are—for their needs to be met by the Christ who came to meet us at the crossroads of our desperate need and His abundant provision. But to receive, we have to be willing to admit our own unedited, unfiltered needs.

When last did you feel close or comfortable with someone because of how impressive they were? Isn't it the people who let us see them at their unbrushed hair, everyday ordinary that make us feel the most at home? Because we can exhale and let down our own attempts to impress and let our real, vulnerable selves out into the open. Much like changing out of those too-tight, skinny jeans and exhaling into a pair of sweatpants. Surely we can do this with our friendships, if we want them to fit us; if we want to fit them.

Friendship Challenge

Complete this sentence and then choose at least one person to put it into practice with this week.

I want to offer _____
to the girls around me, so I'm going to have
to _____.

Here, I'll go first: I want to offer an assurance that the everyday things they're doing are significant kingdom work, so I'm going to have to let them see my life right there in the middle of those things—even on the days it feels messy or uncool—if I want to reflect God's view of the extraordinary right there in the middle of the ordinary.

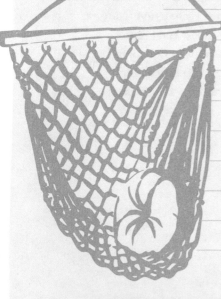

DAY 3

DARE TO STAY WHEN THE GOING GETS TOUGH

If anyone modeled what vulnerability looks like, it would have to be Jesus. Leaving behind the security of heaven, of His title, His throne, His position, He let Himself be delivered naked into the world of poverty and constant misunderstanding and humiliation. In an age when Caesars were claiming they were descended from the gods, the God of the universe sent His Son into the world under cover of almost total obscurity.

Caesar Augustus decreed that all people in his kingdom should be registered in their hometowns (Luke 2:1). Augustus was known as Gaius Octavius or Octavian until about 27 BC. The Roman senate actually gave him the name *Augustus*, meaning honored and dignified, and recognized him as the "supreme leader of Rome."[4] Being named as the Roman emperor gave Augusts the status of a god.[5] While Augustus accomplished many great things for his kingdom and established many policies that contributed to a greater peace and stability throughout the Roman Empire, his rule and his peace would not compare to that of the King born into humble circumstances in Bethlehem.[6]

The tension and choice that existed then is still true for us today—which king will we choose to serve, to follow, to believe? Because friendship with Jesus promises the exact opposite of comfort, luxury, or position—the promises that our culture advertises. Instead, friendship with Jesus is a lifelong lesson in vulnerability. The kind that hurts. The kind that teaches us to stoop lower, to serve longer, to lean into brokenness instead of trying to avoid it. The closer our friendship grows to Jesus, the more we will feel the weight of the cross that He has asked us to carry alongside Him cutting into our shoulders.

> Then Jesus said to his disciples, "If anyone wants to follow after me, let him deny himself, take up his cross, and follow me."
> —MATTHEW 16:24

The kind of vulnerability that Christ asks of us might literally cost us our lives. It will certainly cost us our egos, our self-centered plans, our determination to get our own way, and to control our own image management. Jesus constantly exposes what's really going on in our greedy, self-involved hearts, because He is not fooled by the layers of words and pixels we try to use to disguise our true motives.

And we're not the first to have to face that unmasking.

After Jesus fed the 5,000, the crowds continued to follow Him, but He was quick to point out their motivation.

> Jesus answered, "Truly I tell you, you are looking for me, not because you saw the signs, but because you ate the loaves and were filled."
> —JOHN 6:26

They couldn't think beyond their own bellies—they were following Him for the free food He had provided only a few verses earlier! But what Jesus offered them was Himself. "I am the bread of life" (v. 35), He told them.

READ JOHN 6:35 and fill in the blanks to see what Jesus promises us.

"No one who comes to me will ever be _hungry_, and no one who believes in me will ever be _thirsty_ again."

God Himself is always the answer to what we need. Whether it's food or life. Just like Jesus offered Himself, as the resurrection and the life to Mary and Martha He also offered Himself as the living bread to His followers. Whereas the bread He'd multiplied for them and the manna that had come down from heaven to feed their ancestors wouldn't be able to defeat the inevitability of hunger and death, Jesus promises that people who are willing to eat the bread of life He is offering in Himself will live forever.

But that kind of relationship, that kind of trust, it's uncomfortable. It's not instant gratification. It requires investing parts of our ourselves instead of simply stuffing and numbing ourselves. It requires taking what Jesus is offering and digesting it until it becomes part of who we are, from the inside out. And the people were quick to point that out:

"This teaching is hard. Who can accept it? ... From that moment many of his disciples turned back and no longer accompanied him." —JOHN 6:60,66

They quit following Jesus and His uncomfortable teachings that want to get up in our business and change us from the inside out instead of just satisfying our cravings. But then came Jesus' question to His twelve remaining disciples that rings full and rich with it's own human vulnerability along with a holy challenge:

So Jesus said to the Twelve, "You don't want to go away too, do you?" —JOHN 6:67

I can hear the incredible vulnerability of a man afraid to lose His friends. But we also can't miss hearing the challenge from the God who doesn't want to lose our souls. It's twofold:

1. He is testing who we take our identity from. Who do we listen to?
2. He is testing the condition of our hearts. What do we want?

Listen to how one Bible commentary describes these verses:

The question they raise reveals their real problem: *This is a hard teaching. Who can accept it?* (v. John 6:60). This is a profound question that points to their own hearts. By saying *Who can accept it?* they suggest they are not to blame, that this is too much for anyone to accept. But in fact it shows that they are not humbly docile, as true disciples in this Gospel are. A mark of docility is the ability and willingness to listen and receive. In this Gospel one's identity is known by whom one can and does listen to. [7]

In other words, your identity is who you can and will listen to. When you refuse to listen or say it's too difficult to listen to Jesus, you're refusing to draw your identity from Jesus.

Again let's go deeper with the commentary:

> God knows the condition of our hearts and sends circumstances that will reveal our hearts to us. How do we respond to such exposure? Does it drive us to despair or to deeper dependency upon the Lord? ... So Jesus issues another challenging question, this time to the Twelve: *You do not want to leave too, do you?* (v. John 6:67). This question tests the heart, like the earlier one did (v. John 6:61). ... They must make a choice then and there. Since Jesus knows people's interior dispositions (v. John 6:64; cf. John 2:25), he would know of their faith, so his question tests their hearts and reveals their response to themselves and to one another.[8]

In other words, what do they really want—food or faith? Sustenance or Jesus? Same goes for us. When our hearts are hurting, what do we really want? To numb the pain or to trust that it is being used in our lives by a good God that we can trust?

How did Peter answer (vv. 68-69)? Record this answer in your own words, as if Jesus asked you the same question.

I would go with him
if my family did.

With honesty, Peter put into words my own lonely heart. *Where else would I possibly go? Who else would I possibly believe? Despite my doubts and the days I wish I could keep hiding or pretending, who else promises bread that transcends life and life that can't be smothered in the various graves that call my name—fear, doubt, insecurity, anxiety, worry, envy, and panic?*

No, I'm with Peter. There's nowhere else trustworthy to go. If the choice is hiding my vulnerability in food, or perfectly crafted images of my life on Instagram, or pretending I'm the version of me that I think everyone expects versus handing my entire vulnerable self over to Jesus to cover me, welcome me, and name me as His own, I choose Jesus.

Friendship Challenge

Identify at least one area in your life where you've come to rely on instant gratification to numb your hungers instead of facing your own vulnerabilities.

Now identify one practical action you're going to take this week to replace that numbing behavior with the bread of life from Jesus.

School when I Say the wrong things

We can either *either* ENCOURAGE -or- Compare. We can't do both.

#WSYAS

FRIENDSHIP TAKES ENCOURAGEMENT

Adopt the same attitude as that of Christ Jesus.

PHILIPPIANS 2:5

FRIENDSHIP takes enCouragement

How have you seen FOMO (the fear of missing out) affect your relationships?

There is no one better at lying to ourselves than us. How many times have you opened Facebook or Instagram only to catch a glimpse of an event you didn't know was happening in your town and that you weren't invited to? Or that a group of friends went to dinner and didn't even reach out to invite you? How many times have we translated those images into the assumption that it was done on purpose? That the failure to connect or invite or include was because we were somehow found lacking? How often have we jumped from a photograph to a full-page story in our own heads that stars us as the excluded victim?

How have you seen comparison damage relationships? How has comparison affected your own friendships?

It's a spiritual discipline to hear the voice of comparison in your head and not listen to it, not to let it be the boss of you. Comparison wants to come in and steal something from you. When a friend shares something with you, will you encourage her and share in her joys? Or will you let the voice of comparison drown out the potential shared joy and hear only competition? There is more than enough in the kingdom of God for everyone, but Satan doesn't want us to know that. He wants us to believe we must hoard what we've got, always suspicious that someone is trying to steal it from us.

How have you seen competition damage relationships within your groups of friends?

Encouraging others not only lifts up the one being encouraged, but the one doing the encouraging as well. Encouragement works as the antidote to envy, and those words of encouragement can drive out the poison of comparison. Because envious feelings must be replaced with something. When you feel even a shadow of envy, you must stop and intentionally encourage and send grace. You fight feeling with feeling. You cannot feel jealous if you are extending grace and excitement to someone else. Because joy shared is joy multiplied and jealousy neutralized. But even more difficult than encouraging a friend facing hardships is encouraging a friend in their joy while you are facing hardships. It is very difficult to encourage others from a dark place and when things aren't going great for you.

How can we intentionally choose to encourage our friends? Does that encouragement look different when you are not in a place of joy and contentment?

How has social media helped or hurt your friendships?

The heart is deceitful above all things (Jer. 17:9). Envy and comparison are deeper than social media and have been around longer than Facebook or the Internet. We need to take our identity from Christ, not others, Instagram, Facebook, test grades, or our accomplishments. We have worshiped at the altar of inclusion when we were built to worship at the altar of the only living God. We can't do it on our own. We need Jesus to replace our shrunken, self-centered hearts with His own wildly generous, others-centered drumbeat. But God is a heart-knower, and He can liberate us from our hearts poisoned by the enemy's lies. We need to align our focus not on ourselves, but on what God is doing in other's lives and how we can align ourselves with God's will.

Pray about your own relationships with your friends. Ask God to help you focus on what He's called you to do and to help you appreciate the work He's doing in your friends' lives.

READ PHILIPPIANS 2:5-8 and journal your answers to the following questions:

- What should our attitude be when we begin to feel our own sense of entitlement?
- How do we silence envy by choosing deliberately to encourage our friends?
- If Jesus puts His own pure heart in your body, will it take?
- Are you listening to His messages of dying to self or are you listening to the messages of entitlement?

When JoJo got a lead role in a dance and got to dance with omar. I really wanted it though. I hid my sadness, and tryed to be happy for JoJo

ASK GOD FOR A HEART TRANSPLANT

OK, I'll be blunt with you. This week might sting a bit. Because jealousy is not a fun topic to talk about. And because of all the sneaky, subtle ways a friendship can disintegrate, comparison must be one of the worst. It dishonors the gift of vulnerability that we know from last week is essential for a friendship to flourish. But we're going to go there. We need to go there. Because we don't want the thing your friend is the most excited to share with you to become the thing she wishes she could hide to prevent your jealousy. And on the other hand, we don't want you to unintentionally poke the bear of jealousy in your friends.

It feels like such an embarrassing admission, doesn't it, that we fall down the rabbit hole of comparing ourselves to other people? But it can draw you in and drain the life out of you before you even realize it's happening. And it doesn't seem to have any age limit—we're never too young or too old to get dragged into the sinking sand of comparison.

We live in a world where we can unexpectedly stumble into comparison in seconds, when only moments earlier we were filled up with the contentment of our own lives. Just last weekend I stood at the door of our living room watching my people play across the floor. There were piles of laundry and undone dishes. There were blocks and tiny dolls and all the miniature clothes to go with them. It was a mess and it filled me up with a kind of sticky, delicious happiness. All these people were mine to call "home," mine to love, mine to do life with in this house tucked behind a row of pine trees.

I was so full of the kind of love that surprises us on the best kind of ordinary days that I couldn't move. I just stood in awe, watching the wonder of my life play out before my eyes. The kind of wonder I never could have explained to my teenage self who was so set on being cool and fitting in. The kind of wonder that comes from seeing enough of the broken parts of life to recognize the moments that are highlighted by the tender light of everyday miracles. I took a photo so that I could remember it and then turned back down the hall to our bedroom because the ultimate miracle was that my family had sent me to enjoy a Saturday afternoon nap.

As I climbed into bed, I reached for my phone to set an alarm. But then I made the mistake of opening Instagram. And right before my very eyes I watched my little cocoon of contentment explode into a million pieces of discontent. I scrolled through photo after photo of women who'd been invited to a retreat I didn't even know about—authors who were writing profound words while I had my hair in a dirty ponytail and was still wearing my pajamas. Just like that, I felt comparison shatter all of my delight and satisfaction into miserable shards of envy. It literally took seconds. In breath I was as fulfilled by my life as I'd ever been, and with the next breath I gasped out the miserable grumblings of a toddler who sits surrounded by piles of presents, obsessed over the one thing she didn't get.

Victims of comparison attacks litter the Internet, our sports teams, our study groups, Facebook updates, churches, and circles of friends. We live in a world where there are virtual warehouses of new ways we can find to covet our friend's house, family, and life these days. Nothing is as terrifying as thinking you don't matter because you can't do it like her.

> When have you experienced a moment of "unexpected comparison"? List some of the feelings that dug into your heart in that moment.

One of the best ways to neutralize our effectiveness in the kingdom of God is for us to be tricked into thinking that we don't count. To give up, to sit down, to call it quits, to cry on frustrating afternoons that if we can't do it just like her, then it's not worth doing it at all. Because, in the words of Priscilla Shirer, the enemy would "rather conspire to keep you in a constant state of mourning, grieving over who you wish you were, instead of relishing who you really are, exacerbated by insecurity and crippled by self doubt."[1]

No wonder this desperate, self-centered desire is at the root of every single other sin.

> Christian philosopher Francis Schaeffer says that every one of the Ten Commandments can be summed up in the last: "You shall not covet" (Ex. 20:17). He states, "Anytime that we break one of the other commandments of God, it means that we have already broken this commandment, in coveting."[2]

Ouch. That's a tough one to hear. Are you brave enough to join me in recognizing the places in our lives where the enemy is lying to us? Where he's trying to convince us that if we aren't like her then we don't count?

Let's take a deep breath and write down a few of those tender spots. The places where we worry we don't count because we have felt counted out.

> Take time and think about the last week or the last month—who have you compared yourself to and why? Let's start there so we can start to unmask the lies that we've been sold. Fill in these blanks. You don't need to use names—you can just describe who it is you ache to be like. For example, girls who are popular and loved by everyone, the girl with straight As who knows the answer to every question, the school athlete who can rock at any sport, or the girl at church who is involved in every youth event and mission team project:
>
> I've been comparing myself to _____ because:

I'm often surprised how easily I believe the thoughts that flutter through my head. How I treat them like gospel. But the true Scriptures tell us that,

> The heart is more deceitful than anything else, and incurable—who can understand it? —JEREMIAH 17:9

Ouch again. When last did you question your own heart? Your motives for the comparison or jealousy you're feeling? When last did you pry into what's behind those feelings to get to the root of where they're coming from?

> Rewrite Jeremiah 17:9 in your own words.

> Here's my attempt: My *heart is a big fat greedy liar that wants all the things everyone else has. Whether they're a good fit for me or not. Whether I even have the time for them or not. It's literally impossible for me to fix that myself. I need help. Who can help me?*

It's painful to admit, but there really is no one better at lying to ourselves than ourselves. How many times have you opened Facebook or Instagram only to catch a glimpse of an event you weren't invited to and resented the girls in the picture? How many times have we secretly been disappointed by the good news of others? How many times have we gone home and cried frustrated tears that we weren't the ones chosen, who made the team, who were asked to the dance, who made straight As?

How many times have we translated those images into the assumption that the failure to connect or invite or include was because we were somehow found lacking? How often have we jumped from a photograph in a Facebook stream to a full-page story in our own heads that stars us as the excluded, overlooked, underappreciated victim? It's a dangerous role to play. Just listen to how Scripture describes the effect that kind of envy has on our hearts:

> But if you have bitter envy and selfish ambition in your heart, don't boast and deny the truth. Such wisdom does not come down from above but is earthly, unspiritual, demonic. For where there is envy and selfish ambition, there is disorder and every evil practice. —JAMES 3:14-16

Isn't it interesting that James knows how experienced we are in the fine art of self-deception. Making it almost impossible for us to recognize our own "envy and selfish ambition." We pretend. We deny the truth. We go about our days and our classes and our activities, and it becomes almost an unconscious decision to avoid her calls, ignore her messages, or to scroll past her Facebook statuses without leaving a comment.

That's the noose of comparison and envy tightening around your neck without you even realizing it. Until it's hard to swallow past that lump of dissatisfaction that grows bigger and bigger every time you think about that friend and how "unfair" it is that she has what you want. We might be shocked if someone actually read our thoughts out loud, because we're so good at pretending we're not really thinking them, not really feeling all that terrible anger toward the person who has what we think should be ours.

Go back and re-read how James described this kind of behavior, this so-called "wisdom." What three words did he use to describe wisdom (v. 15)?

In words that should send chills down our spines, James told us that where that kind of envy and selfish ambition exist, two things occur:

I don't know about you but those verses terrify me, because I'm so casual with my comparison. It's so normal to make a hundred different comparisons a day—to other girls' houses, families, grades, art, shoes, purses, body types, messy buns, eyeliner, or the way they wear their skinny jeans. It only takes one of these to sink deep enough into my definition of how I see myself for it to get a grip on my heart and start to poison my mind and our friendship.

And once the lie bites, the slow trickle of poison begins to build up in our veins—a steady drip of toxic comparison that builds up over time and poisons friendships:

> Envy leads not only to foolish decisions, but it blocks the ability to weep with those who weep and rejoice with those who rejoice.[3]

It's impossible to compare *and* encourage. We can either love *or* compete. We can either empathize *or* resent. We can either celebrate *or* sulk. We can't do both.

But there is hope. God is a heart-knower, and He can liberate us from our hearts poisoned by the enemy's lies.

> "I the LORD search the heart and examine the mind."
> —JEREMIAH 17:10 (NIV)

The Great Physician, the Great Healer, the Tender Psychologist has the antidote to the lies we believe if we'll only let Him treat us. David—the shepherd, the youngest of seven sons, the man who spent almost half of his life running away from jealousy that was trying to kill him—said, "You delight in truth in the inward being, and you teach me wisdom in the secret heart" (Ps. 51:6, ESV). Jesus, "the way, the truth, and the life," (John 14:6) is the only One who can open up your secret heart and gently extract the fangs of poison that are lodged there. The only One who can decapitate the lie wrapped tight around our poor, gasping hearts. He has promised that He will and we can hold Him to it. Here is the rescue verse, the verse we can cling to like a life preserver on the days we're drowning in our own jealousy:

> "I will give you a new heart and put a new spirit within you;
> I will remove your heart of stone and give you a heart of flesh."
> —EZEKIEL 36:26

Rewrite Ezekiel 36:26 using your own words.

Here's my version: *I will give you a heart that hasn't been soaked in the poison of comparison. I will put a fresh wind, a new spirit, a life-giving delight right into the very center of who you are. I will rescue you from your heart of stone—the heart that wants to drag you down to the bottom of the ocean and drown you in jealousy. And I will give you a fresh heart beating with the knowledge and wisdom of the Lord. Beating so hard with God's love for your neighbors you'll feel it pounding through every part of your soul and every ordinary conversation.*

Jesus is the only one who can give us hearts of truth, hearts of flesh, hearts that aren't poisoned beyond recognition by the lie that we deserve what she's got. Hearts that He calls by name and that believe they are seen.

Because if we ask Him, Jesus will rip His own bloody and still beating heart out of His chest and graft it into ours. He will give us all of Himself to give us a chance at life—desperate and daring rescue. And then the waiting will begin to see if the new heart will take or if we'll reject it.

And Christ, the greatest heart surgeon, will give us the balm of the Holy Spirit to oversee the grafting process. But ultimately, what we bring into that holy sanctuary of our new beating heart will determine if it lives or if we die.

Tim Keller teaches that what we put in our "hallowed place" is what will define us. He said, "By giving God the praise He deserves, we will heal our worldview as well as our souls."[4] In other words, if we want our new hearts to survive the transplant, we have to demote out of our hallowed places our obsession with others and what they've got versus what we think we deserve. We have to get our obsession with how we compare to others *out* of the hallowed place—stop worshiping at the altar of self when we were built to worship at the altar of the only living God.

And then as the new heart does its work, pumping life and truth through us, hurt from exclusion and comparison will be drowned out by a new message:

> But the fruit of the Spirit is love, joy, peace, patience, kindness, goodness, faithfulness, gentleness, and self-control. The law is not against such things. Now those who belong to Christ Jesus have crucified the flesh with its passions and desires. If we live by the Spirit, let us also keep in step with the Spirit. Let us not become conceited, provoking one another, envying one another. —GALATIANS 5:22-26

Friendship Challenge

It's time to uproot those lies that are trying to strangle our hearts, friends. Let's make two lists. First, go ahead and list all the things you've been jealous that God has given to others. Now, one by one, cross them out. Write next to them the fruit of the spirit from Galatians 5:22-26. This is the drumbeat of our new, Jesus hearts. This is how we get set free.

WHAT GOD HAS GIVEN TO OTHERS	THE FRUIT OF THE SPIRIT

DAY 2

BEWARE! COMPARISON WILL KILL YOU EVERY TIME

A few years back, I was at a conference standing around chatting with several women—old friends and new—and we got to talking about friendship. About walking the difficult line of cheering for our sisters while secretly craving their success. Many of the women turned to me and exclaimed how good I am at this encouragement thing. Like it comes naturally. Like maybe it's easier for me. And I was stunned.

If only they could see inside my head. If only they could tune into my internal monologue. If only they knew about my late nights trying to talk myself off the ledge of thinking myself a worthless waste of time because I didn't do it like her, accomplish it in the same amount of time as them, or get recognized by that group.

There is a dark thing that hides at the fringes of my faith. I can feel it there. Lurking in the shadows. Waiting.

> WAITING for the unkind words from someone I go to school with, play in the band with, or who is a part of my small group.

> WAITING for the Instagram stream that is prettier, and has more followers, likes, and comments than mine to catch my attention.

> WAITING for the updates from the girl who's constantly going on dates, has multiple invites to prom, and is in the running for homecoming queen.

> WAITING for the friend who studies more and makes better grades than me.

> WAITING for the car that is newer, has less dents and scratches, and runs better than mine.

> WAITING for the opportunity or invitation that is more glamorous, desirable, more interesting than mine.

And in that moment, I feel it slink out of the shadows and onto my shoulder. Gently it strokes my hair, caresses my neck, and begins to whisper in my ear.

It whispers, "Unfair. Poor you. You *deserve* more." It understands me. It pets me. It tells me, "You *should* be angry. It's your *right* to feel frustrated. They don't know how *tough* you have it."

It offers me the opportunity to rant and sulk and feel justified in doing so. More often than I care to admit, I have allowed the dark thing to cover my mouth with a strong hand and speak petty words on my mute behalf. It is never pretty. And it is not even original.

This is a lie that has been trying to strangle us since the beginning of time. Since Eve believed that she deserved to, "be like God, knowing good and evil" (Gen. 3:5). This—wanting to be like God, having all that He has—is the essence of entitlement. And we see it woven through the stories of Scripture, none so clearly as in the dysfunctional relationship between King Saul and the up and coming sheep herder and soldier, David. Their twisted and complicated relationship is a 3D example of how comparison and jealousy can literally kill any chance of trust or friendship, no matter how strong the relationship started out.

Take a look at some key points in Saul and David's relationship:

- Saul was impressed with the brave young shepherd who fought the giant Goliath.

- Saul offered David his own armor.

- David defeated Goliath and Saul took David into his household.

- David "was successful in everything Saul sent him to do" (1 Sam. 18:5).

- Saul put David in command of all his soldiers. This pleased everyone.

- GAME CHANGER: The women sang to celebrate the heroes as they returned: "Saul has killed his thousands, but David his tens of thousands" (1 Sam. 18:7).

- Saul's anger exploded. He was furious. He resented the song and David. He complained that the people liked David more than him. His jealousy became terminal.

- Saul had begun the pattern that would continue for the next several decades of trying to kill David and then feeling bad about it, only to have his jealousy boil over again and again until it became his defining character trait.

- Saul was never able to kick the jealousy habit.

Maybe you, like me, have grown up with the story of these two men, watching it unfold on our coloring pages in Sunday School. Maybe we're too comfortable with it. Maybe we need a refresher that this terrible tale of the crippling effects of jealousy tore apart two friends and nearly an entire kingdom. Saul was completely obsessed and crippled by his jealousy. In the words of Drs. Cloud and Townsend in their book, *Safe People*, in Satan's kingdom we are tempted by our envy—our discontentment:

> All of us are tainted with envy. Envy is intimately connected with coveting, and is best defined as a tendency to hate other people for having what we want. Envy says, "What is inside me is bad. What is outside me is good. I hate anyone who has something I desire."[5]

Saul's hatred for David is legendary.

Let's count the number of times Saul tries to kill David. Skim through 1 Samuel 18–20; 23; and 26. Saul came close to killing David around _____ times.

In what ways did Saul attempt to kill David?

That kind of behavior sounds extreme, doesn't it? That sounds a million miles away from our modern, ordinary lives where we know how to be polite and how to congratulate people and often don't recognize the quiet resentment building in our souls toward other people. But this hatred that grows out of the seed of jealousy spreads within the dark places of our hearts just like it did all throughout the Old Testament: Cain killed Abel because his brother got the recognition for a sacrifice that Cain thought he deserved (Gen. 4). Joseph's brothers wanted him dead because they hated that their father loved him best (Gen. 37). Rachel resented Leah for the children she so easily conceived, and they both dragged their servant girls into their bitter feuding over who had more kids, more affection, more status (Gen. 30:1-22).

And we are fools if we think that we don't share the murderous DNA of our spiritual ancestors.

And so, even in our polite world today—without a single confrontation, without raised voices or even a conscious acknowledgment of what's happening—a friendship can be decimated by the simple build up of a toxic and insurmountable wall of jealousy that is deadly. Every time our friend tries to reach out or connect, she smacks into the invisible wall we've built between her opportunity and our jealousy. After a while, she stops trying. And then we get to be angry with her all over again for abandoning us.

This is the terrible, destructive power of what envy breeds. Drs. Cloud and Townsend explain it this way:

> Envy makes us resent people who have something we don't have. It feeds on itself and is ultimately self-destructive. When we envy, the very people who are loving, safe, and generous become the bad guys in our eyes.[6]

Instead of becoming his greatest ally and most trusted general, David became Saul's obsession and threat. And a thousand years later David's most famous descendant, Jesus, walked in His ancestor's footsteps with jealousy dogging His every step.

> The Spirit of the Lord is on me,
> because he has anointed me
> to preach good news to the poor.
> He has sent me
> to proclaim release to the captives
> and recovery of sight to the blind,
> to set free the oppressed. —LUKE 4:18

But part of that freedom came at the cost of control to the ruling religious elite. At the time they ruled with prestige, iron fists, and crushing consequences for anyone who couldn't live up to the letter of the law. And Jesus called them on it. Jesus upset their balance of power with His new kingdom that promised freedom from the stranglehold the Pharisees had made of the law and its impossible-to-live-up-to standards:

> Then Jesus spoke to the crowds and to his disciples: "The scribes and the Pharisees are seated in the chair of Moses. Therefore do whatever they tell you, and observe it. But don't do what they do, because they don't practice what they teach. *They tie up heavy loads that are hard to carry and put them on people's shoulders, but they themselves aren't willing to lift a finger to move them.* They do everything to be seen by others: They enlarge their phylacteries and lengthen their tassels. They love the place of honor at banquets, the front seats in the synagogues, greetings in the marketplaces, and to be called 'Rabbi' by people.
>
> "But you are not to be called 'Rabbi,' because you have one Teacher, and you are all brothers and sisters. Do not call anyone on earth your father, because you have one Father, who is in heaven. You are not to be called instructors either, because you have one Instructor, the Messiah. The greatest among you will be your servant. Whoever exalts himself will be humbled, and whoever humbles himself will be exalted.
>
> "Woe to you, scribes and Pharisees, hypocrites! You shut the door of the kingdom of heaven in people's faces. For you don't go in, and you don't allow those entering to go in."
> —MATTHEW 23:1-13 (EMPHASIS MINE)

The envy and rage of the Pharisees boiled over because Jesus was taking from them their status, their respect, and their followers:

> If we let him go on like this, everyone will believe in him, and the Romans will come and take away both our place and our nation. —JOHN 11:48

Where did their jealousy take them? What was the Pharisees' response? (*Hint: Take a look at Matthew 12:14; 26:4; Mark 14:1; Luke 22:2; and John 11:53.*)

In a bizarre twist of fate, who actually recognizes the true motivation that lurks behind the Pharisees' plot to kill Jesus for what it is—blinding jealousy? Read Mark 15:6-10 and identify that character.

What a deep shame I feel when I realize I've walked in those same footsteps, I've obsessed those same thoughts, I've believed those same lies about entitlement, and I've stewed in those same fears that I'm going to lose out. Instead of being women who might mentor us, encourage us, or raise us up, envy turns friends into enemies and sisters into strangers. Our only hope is the God who might have been killed at the hands of envy but was never subject to it:

> Christ died at the hands of envious men that he might deliver men from the same envy that nailed him to the cross. The jealous and malicious, the resentful and bitter, the covetous and the entitled—all of us have hope…because the One delivered up by our envy was raised up by the good pleasure of his Father.[7]

Friendship Challenge

PART 1: Friends, it's time to confess. It's time to get on our faces before God and tell Him how sorry we are for how we've been jealous of His daughters. It's time to honestly admit that we were wrong for wanting what He'd given to them. It's time to say sorry—say sorry to God and, in our hearts, to say sorry to the women we've hurt by our jealousy. Write that prayer here:

_____

_____

_____

_____

_____

_____

_____

_____

_____

_____

_____

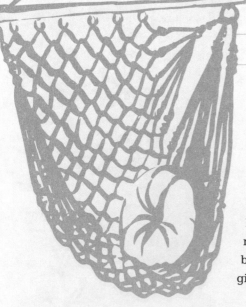

PART 2: Now a quick word of warning about confessing our jealousy. While it is sometimes healthy to confess our sins to the person we've wronged, sometimes it's a case of making ourselves feel better at the expense of making our friends feel worse. This seems to me especially true in the case of jealousy. Confessing jealousy to the person you're jealous of leaves her in a very uncomfortable spot because there's nothing she can do about it—except maybe start to feel bad and horribly self-conscious. She can't unmake her gifts and opportunities, and we shouldn't expect her to.

Confessing our jealousy puts the burden on her instead of where it should be—on us. It unfairly shifts the responsibility to process jealousy in a healthy way from the person in the know to the person who has no clue what's been going on.

So, if we want to bring jealousy out into the light so that the dark creature eating up our hearts can't continue to whisper it's viscous, strangling lies to us anymore, we need a safe friend who's a neutral third party. Confession can be the key to unlock that dark room we pretend doesn't exist. But let's make sure that we process the lie that says, "I don't matter if I don't have what she has" with someone who can't be hurt by that confession.

That kind of holy, challenging conversation doesn't take the friend you've been jealous of hostage. Instead, that kind of conversation with a neutral third party can set you free. And it gives your friend a gift she'll never even know about—the gift of continuing to walk confidently in her calling without doubting herself or being afraid of how it will impact her friendship with you. If you believe you need to confess your jealousy aloud, then ask God to help you find that third party friend who can walk you through that tender process.

PART 3: Finally, a note about guarding our friends against jealousy. There is a time to share our opportunities, accomplishments, and joys. But there's also a time to treasure them in our hearts, happily keeping our contentment to ourselves. This is becoming more and more difficult in a culture that glorifies sharing every tiny detail of our lives, but we can do better. We can remember to guard the hearts of our friends and find tender ways to share news that we know might cause damage to a friend that we love. Surely, the friendship is more significant than the news we're dying to share. Let's keep living Jesus' challenge to die to ourselves, even in our moments of deepest accomplishment and grandest success. Let's die to the temptation to flash our news around like giddy children who don't know any better.

We do know better. And if we love our friends deeply, then we'll be deeply concerned with their well-being and we'll handle our news and their hearts with extra care and consideration. Let's constantly be on the lookout for ways to guard our friendships. Sometimes that starts with what comes out of our own mouths or Instagram streams. Let's take the extra time and care when we're sharing news that we know has the potential to sow comparison and jealousy into a friendship that we hold dear. Let's care more about our friends than our own accomplishments. Let's tread carefully when treading on what we know are the hopes and dreams of the people we hold most dear.

DAY 3

BELIEVE: ENCOURAGEMENT WILL SET YOU FREE

If our goal is healthy, whole hearts, then we need to be ruthless in rooting out our jealousy. And in my experience, simply wishing jealousy away doesn't work. We need to replace it with something substantial, powerful, and life-giving. I believe the antidote to jealousy is a combination of gratitude and encouragement—gratitude for what God has given you and the work He's doing in and through you and encouragement for the work He's doing in and through the lives around you. Choosing to encourage instead of compare is a powerful defensive play, but it doesn't always come easily. It is difficult, deliberate work for every single one of us. So let's get to it.

Comparison is exhausting and self-destructive. The cycle is vicious and viciously effective. And it relies on a lie—the myth of scarcity. Because in Satan's kingdom, where we each want to be our own gods, there is no room for sharing, there is never enough to go around and everything must be grabbed and hoarded to make sure we survive.

But God's kingdom is about abundance, about multiplying, about giving with shocking generosity and still having leftovers.

It's about taking the tiny offerings that our insecure hearts are willing to trust to Jesus and watching as He prays, thanks His Father, and then feeds everyone around us, including ourselves, with those small loaves and fish. His Kingdom breaks and breaks and breaks our own expectations, always multiplying, always offering more, always blessing, in astonishing, unexpected, jaw-dropping ways.

Satan wants you to be discouraged, disengaged, and distracted—he wants you empty, and believing that you're empty of anything to offer. But the carpenter and friend of fishermen who called a motley crew to follow Him and calls you and me each by name, wants all of you, every single breathing bit, to live its fullest, deepest, truest self in His kingdom. And to do that, He will deliberately break us open so that He can multiply all that we have available, all that we can bring to the Kingdom table to feed the people around us.

He's not trying to take something away from us; His intention is to multiply what He's already given us. All that DNA that God has packed with potential and promise, He wants to see shared and spread. It's the ancient promise first spoken to Abram and then passed down through His children all the way to the Messiah and on to each of us, "I will bless you, I will make your name great, and you will be a blessing" (Gen. 12:2).

Take a moment. Look around your room. Think back on your day, and deliberately write down at least five things you have to be thankful for today—five ways God has dumped blessing into your life:

1.

2.

3.

4.

5.

Any blessing that shows up in our lives—from the breath that expands our lungs, the blood that runs through our veins, the best friends who eat popcorn in our living rooms during Netflix binges, the homework that waits at the end of every long school day, or the people who gather around our dining room tables and call us family—every single one of these is a living picture of God's generosity to us. Given to bless us. And intended to bless others. Blessings are not for hoarding, they're for forwarding. Because that is how we reflect God's glory back to Him.

But being able to see beyond our own sense of entitlement, being willing to surrender what *we want* for what *God wants* is not an easy thing. Because if we focus on our own wants, then we're vulnerable to entirely missing what it is that God wants for us. Saul spent almost his entire kingship spectacularly failing to focus on anything beyond himself.

But where Saul failed, his son Jonathan lives on in history as probably the most selfless, others-focused friend ever recorded. And the hallmark of Jonathan's friendship and devotion to David was his relationship to and understanding of God. Even though Jonathan had rights to the kingship, he recognized the Lord's plan to anoint David as king, so he and trusted and lifted up David over himself. As the heir to Israel's throne, Jonathan had every right to have his own agenda, instead, he pursued the Lord's and befriended David.

One commentary paints the picture that unfolds throughout the book of 1 Samuel for us:

> Jonathan was heir to the throne. His brilliant victory over the Philistines (chap. 14) and his nobility of character were good evidence that he would have made a worthy king. But he had found out that God had ordained David to be king, and his graceful self-effacement in giving up his succession to the throne and his unselfish devotion to David, whom he could have hated as a rival, form one of the noblest stories of friendship in history. Jonathan initiated a covenant with David, symbolized by the giving of robe, tunic, sword, bow, and belt. This act reflected Jonathan's recognition that David would take Jonathan's place as Saul's successor.[8]

Jonathan actively worked to advance the work God was doing in and through David's life. He was able to ditch the giant chip of entitlement that his father carried everywhere to put his own agenda aside and lift up the one God had placed in front of him. I want so much to be the friend who lifts up others because I see God's will in their lives. I don't want to miss that kind of holy assignment.

During David's darkest days, Jonathan—the man who could have been his chief competitor—was always there to encourage him. David had gone from being the most popular man in the kingdom to having a price put on his head. He was driven to live like a fugitive, hunted, ambushed, betrayed, forced away from his family and friends, and compelled to live with blood on his hands from the slaughter of those who tried to help him along the way (1 Sam. 22:6-19). He couldn't be sure of anyone—he even doubted members of his own family. And once again Saul was back on his trail with a ruthless, senseless obsession to exterminate him.

It was into this unique and desperate moment that his friend Jonathan risked his own life to bring David encouragement:

> Then Saul's son Jonathan came to David in Horesh and encouraged him in his faith in God, saying, "Don't be afraid, for my father Saul will never lay a hand on you. You yourself will be king over Israel, and I'll be your second-in-command. Even my father Saul knows it is true." Then the two of them made a covenant in the LORD's presence. Afterward, David remained in Horesh, while Jonathan went home. —1 SAMUEL 23:16-17

Highlight the specific actions Jonathan took to encourage David.

Use a different color to highlight the specific words for future encouragement Jonathan spoke over David.

In one breath Jonathan affirmed God's call on David's life, assured David of his support, and made it clear that his allegiance wasn't a secret. Even his murderous father knew Jonathan's loyalties lie with David.

At what must have been one of David's lowest moments, Jonathan was there to keep reminding him what God called him to do and how he was going to get there. He didn't take advantage of David's doubts and despairs to swoop in and snatch up what should have been his. No, where Saul was blinded by his jealousy, Jonathan was guided by his unwavering service to the Lord's anointed.

Now, if you're like me, thinking like Jonathan doesn't just come naturally to us. Instead, we're susceptible to thinking, "But why can't *I* be the anointed one?" Yes? Have you felt like that before?

But here's the thing: You are. You are actually already an anointed one. How's that for a game-changer?

Just as Samuel anointed David, thousands of years later Jesus, our new High Priest, anoints us with His Holy Spirit. Write out 2 Corinthians 1:21.

Look, there's the same word—*anointed*. The idea of being God's anointed ones came from the custom of anointing someone, such as a prophet or king, whom God would appoint to a role or office. Today, believers are anointed by God to carry out the work He calls us to do.[9]

God's Holy Spirit on us is His mark of permanent calling and evidence of His salvation in our lives. We've been set apart to do the work He sets before us. We have been anointed to serve in God's kingdom—here and now—alongside others who have also been anointed and called. And that specifically includes the people in our lives who we've been given as friends. We've been called to lift up the exhausted arms of the people put in our lives on purpose. We've been anointed to serve our friends, just as Jesus served His, just like Jonathan served David. So let's get to it, eh?

Friendship Challenge

1. List the names of at least two friends. More if you'd like!

2. Next, under each name jot down what you understand is God's calling on their lives.

3. Now, under that record at least one way you can encourage and champion their work in a practical way this week.

4. Repeat regularly.

girls aren't hungry for perfection, they're hungry for connection.

FRIENDSHIP TAKES SERVICE

Whoever wants to become great among you must be your servant, and whoever wants to be first among you must be your slave; just as the Son of Man did not come to be served, but to serve, and to give his life as a ransom for many.

MATTHEW 20:26-28

Friendship takes Service

Being the new girl in a room full of old friends can be scary. You may have to act first and be the one to reach out and start conversations in order to begin building relationships. If the opposite is true, if you're the foundation of your group of friends, take a step back to make space in your circle for the new girl. This won't always lead to finding your new best friend but it could be the moment when you open the doors for deeper community.

When have you seen the courage of "going first," or initiating friendship, pay off in your own life or for someone you know?

Do you ever look across the row in church and see the cool girl that you're afraid to talk to? The girl you think would never want to be your friend because she is too cool for you. And she already has friends, and they already have a group, so she won't have room for you. Well here's the thing—there are no cool kids. Period. Every girl is just as insecure and afraid to reach out as you. Don't waste time and miss opportunities to create new friendships because the girl across the aisle has the perfect messy bun and you think you could never be that cool.

How has the perception of "cool kids" kept you from building relationships with others?

A fear of the cool kids is not the only way we can miss an opportunity to build relationships. Have you ever sat at your lunch table and spent the whole time looking over your shoulder at the popular kids' table? Just waiting for them to notice you and invite you over? Or have you ever accepted an invite to hang out a friend's house, and then canceled when someone cooler asked you to hang out instead?

How does this attitude of waiting for something or someone better to come along affect our friendships? Explain how you are missing opportunities to build friendships with the people right in front of you.

READ MATTHEW 20:20-28.

What did Jesus teach His disciples about service?

How should we apply this lesson to our desire to be one of the "cool kids"?

Even Jesus' friends fought over who they would get to sit beside. They each wanted the coolest spot. But Jesus stopped their arguments by saying that to be first, they must act as servants and serve just as He came to serve.

READ LUKE 6:31.

What do we learn about service from this verse?

Rather than just hoping someone will invite you over or wishing that one of the cool girls would talk to you—focus on the friends you already know. Invite the girl from science lab over to your house or ask someone you just met at rehearsals to go out for ice cream. Open the door for conversation by taking the first step toward the people right in front of you. Quit sweating the cool kids and start up your own conversation. Don't let the possibility of awkwardness paralyze you. Instead, take that first small step toward real friendship.

What are some practical ways you can serve your friends? Take time to journal about your friendships and the ways you could be serving them better.

Consider the girls who are not your friends. Is there a first step you can take and overcome your insecurity that is holding you back?

Is there a girl that you can include in your group and get to know better by inviting her for coffee? Pay attention to any opportunities you are missing to engage in community with other girls and take that first step this week to make it happen.

DAY 1

STOP FIGHTING TO FIND A WAY IN

No matter how old we are, I think there's always going to be some part of us desperately wanting to be one of the "cool kids." Define cool however you like, but often we can trace dissatisfied friendships to this search for the elusive "in" and dissatisfaction with where we find ourselves currently: a perceived "out."

The thing we might not realize when we're jealous of the girls sitting at the "popular" table at lunch is that everyone is on the outside of something. But that is only half the story. We are all, each one of us, also on the inside of something—often without even realizing it.

So what we need to learn is that we can either fight to find a way in or we can love on the girls right where we already are. We can obsess over who didn't talk to us or we can focus on the girl right in front of us. We can keep looking for a seat at a more popular table or we can pass the bread and an introduction to the girl sitting right beside us.

This week, we want to remind ourselves that asking someone to save you a seat at her table, only to bypass her because you've spotted a seat at a more popular table can hurt you both. So we're going to teach ourselves to focus on all the *in* that's waiting. All the ways we're wanted. All the ways we belong—if we can stop obsessing over our own wants and start focusing on loving the people around us. Letting people inside our invisible walls. And discovering we've been known and seen by the God who called us *beloved* all along.

As Jonathan served David, so Jesus served His friends. And we are called to follow in those humble footsteps and do the same, serving the people God has placed in our lives. Sometimes the best way to figure out what that looks like is to start with an example of what *not* to do.

Do you remember the show, *What Not To Wear?* I could watch that for hours. It was fascinating to see the transformation that went on when women's eyes were vulnerably and tearfully opened to what clothes were working against them. Stepping into that 360-degree mirror dressing room would not be anyone's idea of fun. But it was only when they truly saw themselves in their clothes from all angles for the first time that the participants started to accept the idea that maybe something needed to change.

I think we experience the same thing when it comes to what we're wearing on our souls. We might think we're motivated by friendship, by encouragement, or by generosity. But sometimes the truth is that we're motivated by entitlement or envy or fear. And we can't actually see all the angles of our motivations until someone holds a mirror up to us, gives us a glimpse of how badly those clothes fit, and offers clear guidelines for what style is intended for our souls instead.

On that note, let's first read a *What Not To Wear* story about soul clothing that is a terrible fit for Jesus' disciples and you and me:

> James and John, the sons of Zebedee, approached Him and said, "Teacher, we want you to do whatever we ask you."
> "What do you want Me to do for you?" he asked them. They answered him, "Allow us to sit at your right and at your left in your glory." Jesus said to them, "You don't know what you're asking."… When the ten disciples heard this, they began to be indignant with James and John. —MARK 10:35-38a,41

In other words, the other ten were flat out furious. How dare these two brothers try and shoulder everyone else out of the way for the prime real estate at Jesus' side?

What soft spot did this behavior hit? Record in your own words what you think James and John were really asking for in this passage and why.

Have you ever done something similar? What happened?

We all do it, don't we? Jockeying for position, for the best seat at the best table. It's the kind of fame grab we are often too subtle, too polite, or too passive aggressive to say out loud. But Jesus hears it nonetheless.

For me, it can sound like, "Please Jesus choose me for that writing assignment, send me to that speaking opportunity, give me that chance to step into the spotlight, light me up with invitations like you've done for her. Set me up on a throne or a headline." It boils down to the same thing, doesn't it?

But Jesus patiently teaches me over and over again how gross that greedy spirit is. And He models His own version of what to wear on our souls and in our friendships.

> Jesus called them over and said to them, "You know that those who are regarded as rulers of the Gentiles lord it over them, and those in high positions act as tyrants over them. But it is not so among you. On the contrary, whoever wants to become great among you will be your servant, and whoever wants to be first among you will be a slave to all. For even the Son of Man did not come to be served, but to serve, and to give his life as a ransom for many." —MARK 10:42-45

And then this one from John—this passage that explodes my head and my heart anytime I read it because the logic is so *completely* other worldly, so impossible for us to grasp—such brilliant teaching through doing that it sinks the lesson deep, deep into our self-centered hearts. In the exact opposite soul clothing that His disciples modeled, this is what Jesus reflects.

> Jesus knew that the Father had given everything into his hands, that he had come from God, and that he was going back to God. So he got up from supper, laid aside his outer clothing, took a towel, and tied it around himself. Next, he poured water into a basin and began to wash his disciples' feet and to dry them with the towel tied around him. —JOHN 13:3-5

What four things did Jesus do in verse 4?
1.

2.

3.

4.

What three things did Jesus do in verse 5?

1.

2.

3.

I can't even read it without tears prickling in my eyes, because it's so humiliating. To be willing to kneel before the sweaty feet of men who spent all day walking dirt roads in sandals, often doubting you and trying to get something from you. And to do it knowing full well what your identity is, how you are descended from kings—both mortal and immortal! The reason this moves me so much is that Jesus humbled Himself *because* He so fully understood where His identity truly lay. All power and glory had been placed in His hands by the Father, but Jesus didn't clench His fists around His heavenly rights. Instead, He opened His hands and released all of His claims to fame, so He could grab a towel and a water basin to wash the dirty feet and serve the broken people in front of Him. After this amazing act of service, look what Jesus did next:

> When Jesus had washed their feet and put on his outer clothing, he reclined again and said to them, "Do you know what I have done for you? You call me Teacher and Lord—and you are speaking rightly, since that is what I am. So if I, your Lord and Teacher, have washed your feet, you also ought to wash one another's feet. For I have given you an example, that you also should do just as I have done for you. Truly I tell you, a servant is not greater than his master, and a messenger is not greater than the one who sent him. If you know these things, you are blessed if you do them." —JOHN 3:12-16

That is how we serve our friends and our own souls. And this is what to wear.

> Therefore, as God's chosen ones, holy and dearly loved, put on compassion, kindness, humility, gentleness, and patience, bearing with one another and forgiving one another if anyone has a grievance against another. Just as the Lord has forgiven you, so you are also to forgive. Above all, put on love, which is the perfect bond of unity. And let the peace of Christ, to which you were also called in one body, rule your hearts. And be thankful. —COLOSSIANS 3:12-15

What does this example teach us to clothe ourselves with? List the various items of soul clothing in these verses.

Friendship Challenge

Consider your friendships this week. Pay attention to the kind of soul clothing you're wearing around them. Let's dream and pretend we have two closets in front of us. On the left side of the page, draw the kind of soul clothes you want to kick out of your closet—the "What not to Wear" in a friendship. Then, on the right side of the page, list the kind of soul clothes you'd like to stock your closet. Because, you can, you know. We only have to ask and Jesus will meet our needs with His own wildly, generous spirit of service.

WHAT NOT TO WEAR IN FRIENDSHIP	WHAT TO WEAR IN FRIENDSHIP

FEED THE PEOPLE AT YOUR TABLE

I don't know about you but when I think about the words service, calling, following Jesus, or discipleship, I don't always think about my refrigerator. Or my desk. Definitely not about my toilet or bathroom. I tend to think far off fuzzy thoughts about adults with important titles, auditoriums, or special TV interviews. And then there's an afternoon when glitter is strewn all over the floor, the counters are covered in cereal bowls, and there has been a steady stream of people through our house by the end of the week and it shows. Then, I remember, that this is what service mostly looks like.

We are everyday ministers of the gospel. It shows up in our lives like neighbor friends who need a ride to school, starting a Bible study with friends, baking cookies for a friend, or even better, talking to the new girl at church. We can become blind to our own ministry that takes place every single day outside the spotlight but is caught in the bright glare of heaven's gaze.

Because that is where we will actually make our names. A name for being the place where our friends feel welcome showing up unannounced. A name for opening the door even when it's inconvenient. A name for making time, giving time, being available. Because our open bedroom doors with clothes sometimes scattered everywhere will be the places we literally practice what we preach before we dare go take that message anywhere else.

I'm not always that good at making this obvious connection. I get irritated and tired, and I like my own personal space. Admittedly, there are days I want to be wanted by important people with important titles more than I want to open my fridge to visitors who know me by name and have seen me in my after school sweat pants. But while I may have those thoughts I don't want them to be the boss of me.

I want my dining room table to be the boss of me—especially when I'm tempted to set my sights on something "better" than my right now, right here friends and neighbors. That table with the big, wide, country planks that have crumbs filling up the cracks. That table with the squeaky chairs we constantly have to repair. That table where we enjoy chatting with the loved ones we invite into our homes. That table that is doing its best work when it's messy and has sticky streaks and an extra bench added down one side. That table and my front door are teaching me that the one seat I need to focus on is the one next to me—not the one across the room or the aisle or even at the other end of the table. It's the seat right next to me right now that is supposed to be my teacher. Whether my best friend, a new friend, a relative, a stranger, or one of my own children is sitting in it.

Dear God, please help us not to miss the beauty of the seat right in front of us. Help us to stop worrying about being impressive and instead to feed the hungry who show up at our tables. To feed them our best, our friendship, our time. To feed them our patience, our interest, our availability. Perhaps our friendships are only as big and deep as our hospitality. And I'm not talking about the size of our rooms or our movie collections. I'm talking about our willingness to invite people in despite the size of our rooms, not because of it.

This is living. Not just the making room for it with clean bedrooms and no clothes on the floor, and toothbrushes put away and sinks wiped down. (*Why on earth can't they ever remember to rinse the sink?* I mutter every night.) No, this is what those spaces are made for. They hold room for the people. And it's the people that make us extraordinary.

These people are always a gift and a living, breathing reminder of the imprint of God left uniquely and divinely on each of them. I have a serving tray in my house that has Hebrews 13:2 painted onto it.

LOOK UP HEBREWS 13:2. Write, paint, or illustrate it.

Now, jot down the names of the people you've come into contact with this week—whether it's your neighbors, your classmates, friends from church, your text messaging group, or the people who live under your roof.

I think I've too often kept one eye on the door, waiting to be amazed by strangers who might come my way. When really it's those I know best—the most familiar and sometimes the most irritating—that I most take for granted that are the most holy representatives of God with us, Immanuel.

When God moved into the neighborhood through His Son, Jesus, He literally became the kid next door, the friend from Temple, the cousin, the brother, the teacher, the best friend, the preacher. He was so ordinary in His regular, everyday roles that it stretched the imagination too much for those who knew Him best to see anything worth paying attention to in His message or His example.

> He went to his hometown and began to teach them in their synagogue, so that they were astonished and said, "Where did this man get this wisdom and these miraculous powers? Isn't this the carpenter's son? Isn't his mother called Mary, and his brothers James, Joseph, Simon, and Judas? And his sisters, aren't they all with us? So where does he get all these things?" And they were offended by him. Jesus said to them, "A prophet is not without honor except in his hometown and in his household." And he did not do many miracles there because of their unbelief.
> —MATTHEW 13:54-58

Don't believe that your people and your place are ordinary, even for a minute. Your life is so full of glory it will weigh you down if you just stop to feel it every once in a while, if you stop to let it sink down deep into your here and now.

I don't want to make the mistake of ignoring the people right in front of me, the people who sometimes show up like neighbor kids with their soccer balls at inconvenient times, and my job is simply to open the front door. I can do this. I'm the only one who can do this because this is my house, I've been given this little plot in God's kingdom, and it's my job to be a good and generous host here. Forget about conferences and stages. If I can't pull out a welcoming chair at my very own dining room table, what business do I have opening a Bible or a book or a message anywhere else?

All through Scripture the central theme from Adam to Noah to Abraham to Ruth to David to Jesus to the disciples to the nations to us is the theme of being redeemed by God for the singular purpose of becoming a witness of that same grace, mercy, and blessing to others. Over and over the promise is given that we are blessed so that we can become a blessing to everyone around us (Gen. 22:17-18). And we can start by simply opening our front doors.

Introduce yourself to the girl sitting next to you. Pay attention to your friends' lives—asking questions, showing interest, taking time to study the people you've long since started taking for granted because you're so familiar with them and their stories. You may be surprised by how deciding to take an extra intentional step toward them today changes things for both of you. Not because there's a crisis or special occasion. Just because you want to connect on purpose.

Friendship Challenge

Who are the people in your life you think you may have been taking for granted lately?

What practical, fun, just-because kind of ways can you reinvest in that relationship?

When did you last feel like the "new girl"?

When did you last have a chance to include a "new girl" in your circle?

If you're currently in a "new girl" season in life, what is one way you can find to show up and connect with your local community to begin plugging in?

If you have a "new girl" in your circle, what practical ways can you deliberately include her this week?

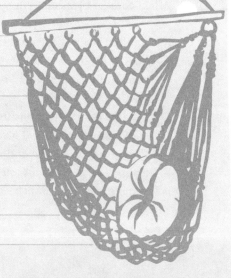

LOVE LIKE YOU WANT TO BE LOVED

Okay here it is—this is the secret to finding and keeping lasting friendships: Become girls who want to see the girls around them flourish.

> Here is a simple rule of thumb for behavior: Ask yourself what you want people to do for you; then grab the initiative and do it for *them*!
> —LUKE 6:31, MSG

They have a word for that in Hebrew—it's *shalom*. But not *shalom* like you might think. Not the overused, under appreciated translation that we're so used to throwing around as the word *peace*. As in the opposite of conflict. Instead, this word is used over 200 times throughout Scripture in a radically more interactive way.

The kind of *shalom* we're challenged to give to the people around us requires us to take an active interest in their physical and spiritual wellbeing. When you look up the various translations to understand how the word is used, *shalom* means caring about someone else's safety and soundness in body, welfare, prosperity, peace and contentment, friendship and good health—to name just a few—as well as caring deeply about seeing conflict come to an end.

Shalom is passionately invested in seeking the wellbeing of others—other people, places, cultures, and neighbors. It's about leaning into the Great Commission to become a blessing to the people around us.

Shalom is a radical word that challenges us to wake up from our obsession with ourselves, instead deliberately choosing to focus on the people around us and desperately caring less about ourselves and more about them.

Let's go on a bit of treasure hunt through Scripture to see how and where the word *shalom* turns up. We'll just sample a few key passages since it's used so many times throughout the Bible and is translated into a variety of English transliterations. The English words *well* and *peace* are just a few examples of how the Hebrew word *shalom* has been transliterated.

Highlight the word *well* every time it appears in the verses. Then, based on the context of the larger story, write in your own words what you think the speaker means when they're using the word *well* in these verses.

"Do you know Laban grandson of Nahor?" Jacob asked them.
They answered, "We know him."
"Is he well?" Jacob asked. —**GENESIS 29:5-6a**

What the speaker means:

And Israel said to Joseph, "Are not your brothers pasturing the flock at Shechem? Come, I will send you to them." And he said to him, "Here I am." So he said to him, "Go now, see if it is well with your brothers and with the flock, and bring me word." —**GENESIS 37:13-14a, ESV**

What the speaker means:

Moses went out to meet his father-in-law and bowed down and kissed him. And they asked each other of their welfare and went into the tent. —**EXODUS 18:7, ESV**

What the speaker means:

And Jesse said to David his son, "Take for your brothers an ephah of this parched grain, and these ten loaves, and carry them quickly to the camp to your brothers. Also take these ten cheeses to the commander of their thousand. See if your brothers are well, and bring some token from them." —**1 SAMUEL 17:17-18, ESV**

What the speaker means:

When the man of God saw her coming, he said to Gehazi his servant, "Look, there is the Shunammite. Run at once to meet her and say to her, 'Is all well with you? Is all well with your husband? Is all well with the child?'" And she answered, "All is well." —**2 KINGS 4:25B-26, ESV**

When Jesse sent his teenage son, David, out from his daily grind among their bleating, flock of sheep to go and check on his brothers who were fighting at the front lines of King Saul's army, he was sending David to check up on their *shalom*—to see how they were doing physically—did they have enough to eat? He also wanted to see how they were doing spiritually—were they discouraged? How was their mood, their sense of hope, their faith in the outcome of the battle?

The same word appears in the New Testament and is also translated *peace*. Highlight the word *peace* where it appears in these verses. In your own words, record what you think the author was trying to communicate by using the word here:

It's the same word that appears as the angels announce Jesus' birth.

"Glory to God in the highest heaven, and peace on earth to people he favors!" —**LUKE 2:14**

What the speaker means:

It's the same word Jesus used in his intimate sermon to His disciples when he told them,

"Blessed are the peacemakers, for they will be called sons of God." — **MATTHEW 5:9**

What the speaker means:

The "*shalom* makers." Those who are invested, interested, and diligently working for the wellbeing of the people around them. The last part of the verse says, "for they will be called sons of God" (Matt. 5:9). Because choosing this demanding and deliberate course of caring about the lives of the people around you, of being a peacemaker, is to walk in the footsteps of the God man, Jesus. The *shalom* maker who actively, deliberately stepped into every day of His life on earth choosing our wellbeing over His own, even past the point when it cost Him His own life.

That's the gospel. We are at peace so we can be peace. We've been invested in so that we can invest.

So, what can you do to find safe, loving, engaged friends who you can trust never to unfriend you? Become radically invested in the people around you. Take the initiative and become that kind of friend first.

Stop keeping score—who called who last, who owes who a text or coffee—and start initiating. Friendship isn't something we passively receive. Friendship is something we actively do. It's a gift we offer for free, not a demand we make with a stamping foot. We love others well because of how well we have been loved ourselves.

READ JOHN 13:34 and record it in your own words.

Friendship Challenge

Jot down the names of two girls you care about. It doesn't even matter if they are your close friends or not.

Now, note two specific ways you can invest in their *shalom*—their wellbeing. Get down to the nitty gritty. What do they need in their lives to flourish, to draw closer to God, and to become the person God created them to be? How can you help facilitate that this week?

Here are some ideas to kick off your own brainstorming about how you can serve and support your friends:

- Send her a text message or note listing specific ways you see her walking in her calling.

- Ask her one practical way you can encourage her this week—does she need help with homework, a friend to pray with, a chance to talk through an idea with someone?

- Is there a gift you could give her that shows how much you believe in who she is in the Lord—a journal, a gift card to Starbucks to use while she's writing, fancy pens to use in her journal?

- How can you publicly share with other friends the work she has done or is doing that you're so proud of?

Without forgiveness, friendship becomes
EXTINCT

#WSYAS

FRIENDSHIP TAKES FORGIVENESS

If anyone says, "I love God," and yet hates his brother or sister, he is a liar. For the person who does not love his brother or sister whom he has seen cannot love God whom he has not seen.

1 JOHN 4:20

Friendship takes Forgiveness

Because there are no perfect people, inevitably someone will hurt us and we will hurt them. What matters is what comes next. Will we forgive them, or will we withdraw? Will we work it out, or will we write it off? We are all broken and wounded, but only by choosing to stay can we start to grow deep roots.

How have you seen past relationships affect your current relationships?

Are you carrying any baggage from past friendships into new ones? Sometimes it's too late once we finally realize we're overreacting to a situation because of past hurts. Satan would love to see us poison every new relationship with the pain we carry from old relationships.

READ 1 JOHN 4:20.

What does this verse reveal about the necessity of forgiveness?

Forgiveness is the first step in moving forward. It's about making peace with the past to create an opportunity for relationships in the future, though not necessarily with the people who've scarred us. But sometimes, by the grace of Christ, forgiveness is exactly that powerful—it restores even the most broken relationships.

Forgiveness does not negate consequences and accountability. It doesn't even imply there will be a healthy relationship going forward, but forgiveness is what sets you free in Christ. When you are set free by Jesus Christ, you are really free (John 8:36)—free from the chains of your sin, free from your shame, and able to freely offer forgiveness to the other person.

How do you see forgiveness as an act of courage? What does it look like to move toward the courageous act of forgiveness?

Choosing forgiveness and acting on it—even when we don't feel the emotions of forgiveness—is not easy. Leading with an act of forgiveness allows the feelings of forgiveness to follow.

Do you feel the Lord calling you to forgive an offense you've struggled to let go of? Discuss with your group some ways you can choose forgiveness and act upon it, even when the feelings aren't behind the action just yet.

Before you are able to forgive, you may first have to grieve the relationship you thought you would have with that person, and accept the relationship that you do have. Acknowledge that you were hurt before moving on to the next stage—forgiveness.

How do you see grief as a part of the forgiveness process?

Forgiveness is a process and sometimes the hurts are so big that you need to ask daily for help. Practice forgiveness every day—the more you practice, the easier it becomes to extend forgiveness that is real, and true, and sure. Forgiveness is for our own benefit too—it's how we find closure even in the relationships that won't ever be completely fixed. Forgiveness removes the hurt so that we can heal. Jesus, the God-man who had more reason to hate, resent, and build up bitterness than most of us, constantly, deliberately, ruthlessly loved those who hurt Him. He constantly chose love over the easier choice of hate. Are we brave enough to follow in His footsteps?

When have you made the difficult choice to give loving forgiveness instead of bitterness and hatred? Describe a situation in which you can choose loving forgiveness now.

Jesus said, "I have come so that they may have life and have it in abundance" (John 10:10b). He's the only one who can cut that dead weight of broken relationships and old patterns off our backs, and invite us into community with Him—setting us free to embrace friendship.

Journal about a time when you thought you had moved past an old hurt only to have unforgiveness reappear in your life. What effect has unforgiveness had on you or others?

DON'T LET YOUR PAST HURTS POISON YOUR CURRENT FRIENDSHIPS

Even if you show up for friendship, even if you open your door and invite people into your real, messy life and make time and welcome interruptions because you meant it when you said you really want friends— friendship can still end up hurting you. More specifically, at some point Christian girls will hurt you—as will non-Christian girls. Hopefully not on purpose. Hopefully through simple ignorance or their own insecurity. But sometimes, sadly, it will have been on purpose. But either way, what then? How do we remain open to friendship when friendship has taken advantage of our vulnerability and hurt us?

Do we close our doors and our hearts or do we keep trusting God and His invitation to love other people and let them in? Because if we haven't been able to trust other people, if they've let us down and if they've hurt us—by accident, or even worse, on purpose—how can we keep putting ourselves out there?

Have you ever been hurt by a friend? What happened?

How do you think that past hurt has affected the friendships you built after that?

I don't know about you, but I have definitely had friendships that left my heart tender and my soul suspicious. When you've been badly wounded by a girl you thought was your friend, I think you're susceptible to a kind of friendship PTSD (post-traumatic stress disorder).

In his book, *Social Intelligence: The New Science of Human Relationships*, Daniel Goleman explains why. Every social interaction reshapes our brains through what is called neuroplasticity. In other words, just like we learn not to touch the candle flame after we get burned the first time or how we might enjoy repeating the habit of late night TV binging and ice cream, repeated social experiences teach us which relationships are hot to the touch and which ones are delicious.[1]

First as little girls and then as teens and adults, the patterns we live over and over again in our friendships aren't by accident. They're the actual rewiring of our brains to connect or not connect based on past experiences. So if we've had a defining relationship that ended up exploding our hearts, we're more likely to experience some degree of post-traumatic stress when we find ourselves in a similar relationship in the future.

The thing is, our friendship distress can be the reason we're missing out on connecting with new friends or going deeper with our current friends. It can be the reason we haul a huge suitcase of friendship baggage along with us every time we walk into the conversation.

I believe if it were up to him, Satan would like nothing more than to see us all infected by our past hurts and the grudges we lug around with us. If it were up to Satan, he would strap all our failed friendships and all those times our trust was disappointed onto our backs and have us carry them into every conversation, every tender connection, and every new interaction, into every Bible study, and study group, and into every girl's night out.

You can cripple a friendship before it even begins by piling the baggage of all our previous relationships onto it. That friendship that ended badly, that misunderstanding, that time you were left out that you can't seem to get over—are you still dragging those around with you? Are those relationships still causing you friendship distress?

Let's pause there for a minute. Let's ask the Holy Spirit to show us what friendship baggage we're still holding onto.

Father,
I trust you with my heart. I trust you with my past. And I ask you to gently show me if there are pieces of my own anger, or disappointment, or hurt that I'm still holding onto from past friendship failures? If you see it, will you help me see it too? So that I can let it go. So that I can stop dragging all that pain into each of my new relationships. Will you please set me free? Will you defuse the memories I'm walking around with and give me a new friendship story?
Amen.

NOW, LET'S READ JOHN 10:10 TOGETHER.

A thief comes only to steal and kill and destroy. I have come so that they may have life and have it in abundance.

What has Jesus promised to bring us?

He's the only one who can cut the dead weight of broken relationships and old patterns off our backs and invite us into community with Him, setting us free to embrace friendship. He is not a stingy God. He is generous in all areas. Why wouldn't He be generous in the area of friendship too?

Read these verses, and describe how each illustrates the generosity of the God we serve.

You prepare a table before me
in the presence of my enemies;
you anoint my head with oil;
my cup overflows.
—PSALM 23:5

God's Generosity:

If you then, who are evil, know how to give good gifts
to your children, how much more will your Father
in heaven give good things to those who ask him.
—MATTHEW 7:11

God's Generosity:

Give, and it will be given to you; a good measure—pressed down, shaken together, and running over—will be poured into your lap. For with the measure you use, it will be measured back to you. —**LUKE 6:38**

God's Generosity:

As much as Jesus understands life and generosity, if anyone understands friendship betrayal, it is also Jesus. Betrayed by one of His own disciples and disowned by His closest friends. These wounds are real. They are raw. But Jesus won't let us stop there. He won't let us live in the place where we're the victims constantly pointing fingers. No, He wants us to follow in His wounded footsteps to the place where we are willing to forgive, because it's the only way through to life.

For you were called to this, because Christ also suffered for you, leaving you an example, that you should follow in his steps. —**1 PETER 2:21**

Then Jesus said to his disciples, "Whoever wants to be my disciple must deny themselves and take up their cross and follow me." —**MATTHEW 16:24, NIV**

That's what this first day is about: simply preparing our hearts to be willing to walk in Jesus' footsteps, because forgiveness is very hard. It may be one of the hardest spiritual disciplines we have to put into practice. And it's not easy to just jump right into it. So today is simply about pausing and recognizing your hurts and preparing your heart for what comes next—either bearing a grudge or accepting Jesus' offer of life and freedom through forgiveness. Those are the only two choices.

Friendship Challenge

Grab a stack of scrap paper, sticky notes, or index cards. Now, remember those past hurts from friendship that the Holy Spirit brought to mind when we prayed earlier and write them down. One per piece of paper. Write down what happened, what was done to you. Be specific about your disappointments. Write down all the ways that you felt let down, or overlooked, or taken for granted by a friend (past or current). Just get it all out—bleed your hurts onto the page.

Now, I want you to read those bits of paper out loud. We bear witness to how you were hurt. We don't discount it. We don't try to brush it off or excuse it. We see it, friend. We see it, and we acknowledge that it hurt. It's OK to cry. It's OK to ache. We'll just sit here together. Take all the time you need.

And once you've caught your breath, tuck those scraps of paper into an envelope and put them into your Bible for safekeeping. We'll come back to them on Day 3, OK? This is how we prepare our hearts for what comes next. This is how we take the first step to being ready to give and receive forgiveness.

BE BRAVE ENOUGH TO ASK FOR FORGIVENESS

Because there are no perfect people, inevitably someone will hurt us and we will hurt someone. What matters is what comes next. Will we forgive them, or will we withdraw? Will we work it out, or will we write it off? We are all broken and each wounded, but only by choosing to say sorry or receive someone else's apology can we start to grow deep roots into a friendship.

Forgiveness is always ground zero when it comes to any relationship, especially friendship. Let's take a moment to think about that.

What are your friendship habits when the going gets tough? Highlight all that apply to you. When you've been hurt by a friend do you:

☐ Cut and run

☐ Dial up the passive aggressive behavior until she realizes something is wrong

☐ Pretend like nothing happened

☐ Confront her—via Facebook, text, or in person

☐ Avoid her until the friendship fades away

☐ Make time to talk it out with her

Now, what about if you're the one who has hurt a friend? Whether it was unintentional or because of your own careless behavior. Whether you believe what you did warrants someone being hurt or not, if she approaches you, what is your response in that situation? Do you (highlight all that apply):

☐ Become defensive

☐ Make excuses and point out all the ways you are also the victim

☐ Ignore the issue

- ☐ Dodge the conversation altogether so she never has a chance to connect with you
- ☐ Take the time to listen, and understand, and ask for forgiveness
- ☐ Feel so bad that the awkwardness interferes with the future of the friendship
- ☐ Decide that the friendship isn't worth "the drama"

Looking at that checklist, it might seem really obvious what the right choices are. But as we all know, real life, real time conversations about hurt can be *hashtag* awkward. They are tough to navigate and tough to come back from, but choosing whether or not to ask for forgiveness or grant forgiveness will make or break a relationship. Literally.

Because we're good at recognizing our own hurts, but can sometimes have a blind spot when it comes to how we've hurt other people, let's start there. Before we move on to what it looks like for us to extend forgiveness, let's spend some time on the more awkward and self-conscious subject of what it looks like for us to ask for forgiveness—what it looks like when we're the ones in the wrong. (If you can't think of a time you've ever been in the wrong in a friendship, then I think this chapter is especially for you).

As I've studied forgiveness over the past year, I've been so struck by the different responses of two of Jesus' disciples to their own friendship failures. Peter and Judas both betrayed Jesus. Both hurt the man they claimed as a friend. Both despaired, both wept, and both wished they could undo what they had done. But one was swallowed up in despair and took his own life, while the other went to Jesus for forgiveness and to have his life restored.

Let's spend some time with these two men. Let's retrace those terrible three days and nights to see how they each responded when confronted with how they'd betrayed their best friend.

Read each of the verses in their timelines and connect the dots of what unfolded during one of the most notorious stories of betrayal of all time. Fill in the blanks with the behaviors of Judas and Peter:

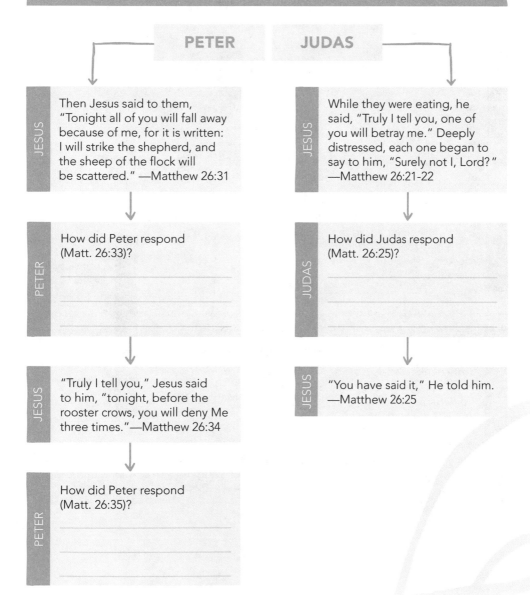

JESUS PREDICTS THE BETRAYAL OF BOTH JUDAS AND PETER

PETER

JUDAS

JESUS
Then Jesus said to them, "Tonight all of you will fall away because of me, for it is written: I will strike the shepherd, and the sheep of the flock will be scattered." —Matthew 26:31

JESUS
While they were eating, he said, "Truly I tell you, one of you will betray me." Deeply distressed, each one began to say to him, "Surely not I, Lord?" —Matthew 26:21-22

PETER
How did Peter respond (Matt. 26:33)?

JUDAS
How did Judas respond (Matt. 26:25)?

JESUS
"Truly I tell you," Jesus said to him, "tonight, before the rooster crows, you will deny Me three times."—Matthew 26:34

JESUS
"You have said it," He told him. —Matthew 26:25

PETER
How did Peter respond (Matt. 26:35)?

JUDAS AND PETER BETRAY JESUS

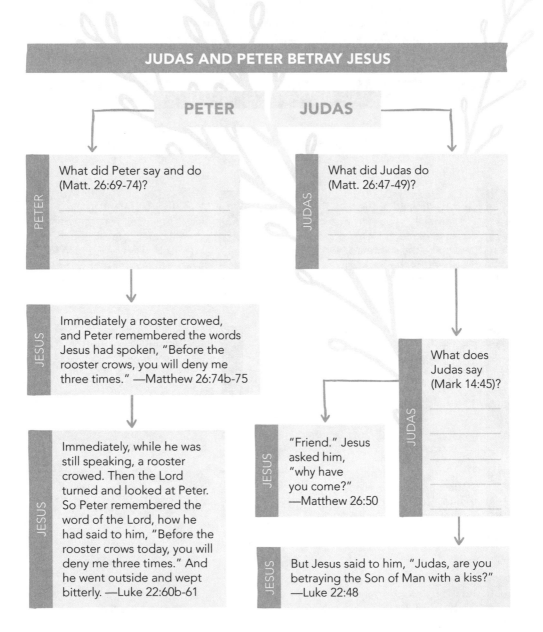

PETER **JUDAS**

PETER | What did Peter say and do (Matt. 26:69-74)?

_____

_____

_____

JUDAS | What did Judas do (Matt. 26:47-49)?

_____

_____

_____

JESUS | Immediately a rooster crowed, and Peter remembered the words Jesus had spoken, "Before the rooster crows, you will deny me three times." —Matthew 26:74b-75

JUDAS | What does Judas say (Mark 14:45)?

_____

_____

_____

_____

JESUS | Immediately, while he was still speaking, a rooster crowed. Then the Lord turned and looked at Peter. So Peter remembered the word of the Lord, how he had said to him, "Before the rooster crows today, you will deny me three times." And he went outside and wept bitterly. —Luke 22:60b-61

JESUS | "Friend." Jesus asked him, "why have you come?" —Matthew 26:50

JESUS | But Jesus said to him, "Judas, are you betraying the Son of Man with a kiss?" —Luke 22:48

JUDAS AND PETER'S REGRET

PETER   JUDAS

PETER

How did Peter respond (Matt. 26:75; Mark 14:72; Luke 22:62)?

_____

_____

JUDAS

What did Judas feel, what did he do, what did he say, and what final choice did he make (Matt. 27:3-5)?

_____

_____

Peter's story did not end here. Why?

_____

_____

Judas' story ends here.

JESUS

Notice how Jesus' messages sent special and specific words to Peter about Jesus' resurrection (Mark 16:5-7). What did they say?

_____

_____

PETER

What did Peter do (John 20:3-8)?

_____

_____

PETER

What did Peter do (John 21:7b)?

_____

_____

JESUS

When daybreak came, Jesus stood on the shore, but the disciples did not know it was Jesus. "Friends," Jesus called to them, "you don't have any fish, do you? "

"No," they answered.

"Cast the net on the right side of the boat," he told them, "and you'll find some." So they did, and they were unable to haul it in because of the large number of fish. The disciple, the one Jesus loved, said to Peter, "It is the Lord!"—John 21:4-7a

JESUS

After Peter denied Jesus three times, what question did Jesus asked Peter three times (John 21:15-17)?

_____

What does all this mean? Is there really some similarity between these two men and their stories? I've become so fascinated by them this year. I've leaned in as close as I could to peer back through the pages of history to try to understand how their betrayals had such radically different endings. And the more I read, the more I study, the more convinced I am that each of their unique plot twists hinge on whether or not they believed that Jesus could and would forgive them. We've retraced their footsteps in the charts, now let's decode what their actions meant.

Without any trace of irony, Jesus called Judas His friend right on the very doorstep of his betrayal (Matt. 26:50). Their was no echo of judgment in Jesus' words. When Jesus used the title of *friend* toward Judas, his greeting was kind, but not intimate.[2] This is simply the honesty of a God who was publicly acknowledging the truth of His own predictions. Eye to eye, cheek to cheek, Judas had to face the truth about himself in Jesus' eyes and words.

And then there's Peter who, as the rooster crowed, looked into the eyes of his friend, the man he swore to defend with his very life, and saw the reflection of his own failure and Jesus' prediction realized. But the commentaries tell us that there wasn't any condemnation in Jesus' gaze. Instead, much like His interaction with Judas, it seems that Jesus felt compassion for Peter:

In describing how the Lord looked at Peter (Luke 22:61), Luke used the same word John used to describe the way Jesus looked at Peter when they first met (John 1:42). It was a look of love and concern.[3]

Both Judas and Peter were devastated. They were crushed. They wept bitterly. They mourned, they grieved, and neither of them tried to defend himself. But here's the crux of the difference between their shockingly different outcomes—Judas was crushed by the weight of his own guilt, and it killed him. But Peter, oh Peter. He went running and splashing, guilt and all, to Jesus.

Judas went to the chief priests and elders for absolution, and when he couldn't get it, he judged himself. And the weight was too terrible to bear. Maybe Judas' terrible act of self-judgment and condemnation has some echoes of familiarity—for those of us who can hardly move for the weight of our own crushing guilt.

How are you enacting judgment on yourself? Do you binge eat? Do you purge? Do you cut? Is there a constant stream of criticism in your head raging against yourself? Friends, it's time to bring all that self-hatred to the One who will forgive you. Stop trying to carry it all by yourself. Stop trying to punish yourself. Stop hating yourself. It's time to make like Peter and run to Jesus. Run as fast as your tired and disappointed legs can carry you to the God of the empty tomb, to the God who carries life in His very bones.

Will we be brave enough to bring our friendship failures, our sins, and selfish behavior to the Savior who can resurrect them? Or will we be crushed by our own disappointments and run away from the friendships that try to make us face them?

Friendship Challenge

Is there something you need to ask forgiveness for? Is there a relational sin that's haunting you? A sin that's crushing you with its weight, that's trying to choke the very life out of you? A careless sin, a sin that hurt a friend and broke a friendship? Bring that sin to Jesus. Don't avoid Him. He already knows. He's already seen.

He's leaned His cheek up close to your own cheek right in the very act of your sinning. Turn and meet His gaze and tell Him you're sorry. It's OK. He loves you. He can radically redeem your life the way He did Peter's. God wants you in His kingdom and He gave His own Son's life to get you there.

Write a prayer to Jesus and ask for forgiveness. Then go and ask forgiveness if you've hurt any of His daughters. Asking forgiveness is an act of courage. Trying to carry, bury, hide, or run from your sins is an act of cowardice. And that never ends well. Come to the God of the empty tomb and let Him wash you clean and send you whole and healthy back into friendship.

IF WE LOVE GOD WE CAN'T
HATE OUR FRIENDS

There is a reason that the Lord's Prayer first talks about asking for forgiveness for ourselves, and then once we're free of our own debts, it moves to forgiving the debts owed against us. In the world of friendships that we want to invest in deeply, asking forgiveness is step one. Then once we've received what we know we didn't deserve, extending the same grace and forgiving the people around us is step two. Because to hate the people around you is to hate the image of God in them. Jesus, the God-man who had more reason to hate, resent, and nurture bitterness than any of us, constantly, deliberately, and ruthlessly loved those who hurt Him and consistently chose love over the easier choice of hate. Are we brave enough to follow in Jesus' footsteps? Because His challenge to love our neighbors as ourselves is intimidating. Because it has resounding ramifications.

Write out 1 John 4:20:

Forgiveness is an act of generosity. It's passing everything that we've freely been given onto someone else. Without forgiveness, friendship becomes extinct and relationship non-existent. In his book about the new science of human relationships, Daniel Goleman calls forgiveness "an antidote" to the "lasting biological consequences" of cycles of rage, hurt, and revenge.[4] Goleman goes even further to say that forgiving someone who has hurt us actually reverses those biological reactions because "it lowers our blood pressure, heart rate, and levels of stress hormones and it lessens our pain and depression."[5]

In my own experience, however, there's something of a sliding scale for how hard it will be to forgive someone. On one end of the scale are the people who hurt us unwittingly. They didn't plan to hurt us. They hurt us by accident, by being careless with our feelings or completely ignorant of what the impact of their actions were. These are the people we trust and who deep down in our gut we know are rooting for our best. And knowing that they never meant to hurt us goes a long way in helping us forgive them.

Describe a situation in which you knew a person accidentally hurt you.

How did you know it was an accident?

Were you able to forgive them easily? Why?

But on the other end of that sliding scale is a dark and wretched place—because there lie the hurts caused by people on purpose. Or by people who were so cavalier with our hearts that even if we tried to show them our open wounds, they'd shrug their shoulders and go back to their coffee.

Beth Moore describes in wrenching words the exact feelings I've had in those situations:

"How often have I made a fool of myself just trying to get someone who hurt me to hear me?"[6]

The deep injustice of being wounded by someone who doesn't care or isn't interested in understanding our pain can feel like acid burning away our skin. We feel stripped, emotionally bare, skin raw and flaming with the unfairness of it all.

On the day I was baptized, I had someone walk up to me and hand me a card. And what I thought was going to be a note full of love and affirmation and finally reconciliation from someone who had haunted my life with misery for months turned out to be a blistering scream of condemnation and ugliness. Handed to me in church. On the day I was publicly dedicating my life to the Lord. Twenty years later I can still feel the impact of that slap.

On the day Joseph was sent out to check on his brothers and bring them word from their father, their hatred boiled over while he was still at a distance. It then grew hands and fingers that stripped off his "robe of many colors" (Gen. 37:23) the moment he arrived and threw him into a deep gash in the earth. After plotting the death of their little brother they casually, "sat down to eat a meal" (Gen. 37:25). The Amplified Bible describes the scene well:

> We saw the distress and anguish of his soul when he begged us [to let him go], yet we would not listen [to his cry]. —GENESIS 42:21, AMP

The terrible injustice of people in your life who move from hurting you to dishing up supper without ever taking a breath in between to say they're sorry can make you sick.

Forgiveness won't be easy, but it will be necessary. And ultimately it will be more satisfying than revenge. Because,

> Forgiveness is not passivity, dear one. It is power. It is the ability to withstand the pressing, quaking gates of hell. Take this power and wield it. It's your right as a child of God. In the power of Jesus, first you will it and soon you'll feel it.[7]

But how? How do we grope our way to forgiveness? Not because we want to or even because we're capable, but only because there are giant footprints we can sink our desperate feet into. We can walk in the shoes of Christ because He did it first. Jesus forgave. While being tortured He looked out into the faces of His torturers and He said the immortal words,

> "Father, forgive them, for they do not know what they are doing." —LUKE 23:34, NIV

This is only possible because forgiveness is not about a feeling, but about a willing. Forgiveness sent Christ to the cross, where He willingly was beaten, spat upon, and nailed by us and for us. The God-man could've said, "Forget this," but instead He bowed His head and generously and unfairly took upon Himself your sin and my sin. And to the ones who had directly hurt Him, He immediately offered forgiveness.

Forgiveness. As Beth Moore wrote, "No stronger force exists."[8]

Christ chose to forgive them—and us—because He knew that they didn't have a clue:

> Whoever threw you into the pit doesn't have any idea how much it hurt you. I'm not sure they would get it even if you told them in detail upon detail. No, they don't have a clue how much it affected your decisions and relationships. Humbly, but very specifically, forgive them not only for their destructive actions, but also for their *ignorance*. You have no other choice if you want out of that pit.[9]

And that's what we want, yes? Out of the pit. Out of the tomb. Out of the gaping mouth of death that would like nothing more than to close it's jaws around us and chew us up. But we were made for life and God wants to give us life—life to the fullest.

Nothing takes more of God's power working through us than forgiveness. Only through Him are we able to forgive.[10]

When have you experienced a hurt you thought you'd never be able to forgive? What happened?

If you've already forgiven those involved, what did you do?

If you haven't forgiven them yet, what steps can you take to forgive them today?

But forgiveness doesn't necessarily imply friendship.

Can you biblically forgive someone without restoring or manufacturing a friendship? Why is this sometimes necessary?

How can forgiving a friendship, even without restoration of that friendship, help you with future relationships?

Forgiveness in friendship "does not require condoning some offensive act, forgetting what happened, or reconciling with the perpetrator. It means finding a way to free oneself from the claws of obsession about the hurt."[11] Forgiveness is making peace with the past so that there is opportunity for relationship in the future. Not necessarily with the same people who've scarred us. But sometimes, by the grace of Christ, forgiveness is exactly that powerful to restore broken relationships to fresh health and offer the same people a completely different way of relating to one another.

Forgiveness is the beginning. And it's how we find closure even on the relationships that won't ever be completely restored to us. Because forgiveness is like a pair of tweezers picking out the shards of shrapnel embedded in our hearts and minds by people we once loved. Forgiveness removes the hurt so that we can heal. Forgiveness is the gift we give to ourselves so that we can stop bleeding and begin to grow new skin over old wounds. Forgiveness is the first step out of the dark and into the light.

Friendship Challenge

Remember our friendship challenge from Day 1 this week—those hurts we wrote down and that you tucked into your Bible for safekeeping? OK, now here's what I want you to do. I want you to find somewhere comfortable to sit. Somewhere you feel safe. Somewhere you won't be interrupted. And I want you to take those bits of paper and broken parts of your heart, and I want you to hold them up in front of you. I want you to tell Jesus what was done to you. Show Him. Let Him see. Read them aloud again if you need to.

You can tell Him it was unfair. He understands unfair from the inside out.

Now close your eyes and just sit there in the presence of the Holy Spirit. What is Jesus doing? Can you sense His presence? My hope is that you will sense how much He loves you. My hope is that you would be able to imagine that if He was in the room with you, He would be standing up, walking over to you, and taking you in His arms to hug you and comfort you.

My friend, now is the time to shred those bits of paper. Shred them up as small as they can go. With Jesus holding tight onto you, I want you to witness all those words being torn down into little bits and pieces. We can't let them have any power over you anymore. They have no power over your life in Christ because He has come to set you free.

Now, if you have a fireplace or fire pit, burn them. Or you can go one of my favorite routes and flush them down the toilet. Or you can burn them and then flush the ashes. I've done both in the past.

> **READ ROMANS 8:31-39.** Write out the verses that comfort you the most in this passage, and receive them as the Holy Spirit speaking wholeness and healing into your most tender and broken places.

_____

_____

_____

_____

_____

_____

_____

_____

_____

Once you have been able to grant forgiveness then we can say with Paul:

> I have been crucified with Christ, and I no longer live, but Christ lives in me. The life I now live in the body, I live by faith in the Son of God, who loved me and gave himself for me. —GALATIANS 2:20

This is my very specific prayer for you today: that you will feel more alive and more free than you have since the day you were first hurt, that you would know and believe that Christ lives in you, and that you have His forgiveness pumping in your veins. I pray for this kind of forgiveness—the kind that doesn't require a friend to ever say the words, "I'm sorry" to you, the kind that heals from the inside out.

It's not our job to Rescue other people; it's our job to love them. it's Jesus' job to Rescue them.

FRIENDSHIP TAKES WALKING AWAY WISELY

If possible, as far as it depends on you, live at peace with everyone.

ROMANS 12:18, NIV

FRIENDSHIP takes WALKING AWAY wisely

READ ROMANS 12:9-21.

If possible, as far as it depends on you, live at peace with everyone.
—ROMANS 12:18

How do we serve and love our friends well? What are the correct boundaries to put around ourselves?

We often end up shouldering the burdens of our friends, because we so badly want to see them healthy and fulfilled. Sometimes we're more invested in their well-being than they are. So what then? How do we love well without being dragged under by the weight of a friendship that's become too heavy and too unhealthy to keep carrying? How do we figure out when to keep trying and when it might be beyond our ability to fix things?

Drawing safe boundary lines doesn't make you selfish, unchristian, or impolite—it makes you wise. And it puts your hope in the right place—in the God who can actually transform and who will not disappoint (Rom. 5:5).

How is having boundaries in a relationship healthy?

What can happen when we don't have boundaries?

As Christians, we're taught that it's a good thing to be willing to "carry one another's burdens" (Gal. 6:2). But being willing to carry our friends' burdens is not the same as being willing to carry their dysfunction, rage, inappropriate behavior, manipulation, passive aggression, cruelty, control, and a whole host of other traits that we can unknowingly inhale like secondhand smoke.

How can you be a friend to someone without fully taking on her burdens?

Sometimes, keeping healthy boundaries means walking away. This is a sad, and frustrating, and painful reality—one that often makes us feel guilty. Especially when we've done all we can to help that friend. We do not run away from or cut out difficult friendships, but we have to be willing to walk away in love. We can forgive and love, but we can't fix. Only Jesus can do that. We can only provide a safe place for our friends to share their burdens when we are in a healthy place ourselves.

Describe to your group an time when the Holy Spirit prompted you to walk away from a friendship or situation.

In friendship, it's easy to begin carrying our friend's burdens, but we aren't meant to carry her load—it's too heavy for us. You can be a friend to someone without carrying her burdens. You might get to a point where you can't find those boundaries, and your friend needs more than you can give her. That doesn't make you a bad friend; it makes you a safe and trusted friend who can help move her toward something better by removing yourself from the situation. A friend may be leaning on you, expecting you to heal her, when in fact the One she needs to lean on is Jesus. Our friends will constantly be dissatisfied if they are coming to us instead of seeking Him to help with their burdens.

How can stepping out of the way lead to transformation in someone's life?

We can't fix everything, and by trying to fix it, we may be getting in the way of what God is trying to do. If you are interfering to the point that you are absorbing all the negative consequences, while your friend never experiences them, there is no opportunity for her to change. If you step out of the way, it creates room for learning and, hopefully, fresh life.

We live in a time and a culture that's obsessed with what other people think of us, and deleting a friendship takes just the swipe of a finger. If you are closed off from a person in every way, then how can there be restoration?

Journal about any relationships that may have broken in an unhealthy way. Did you leave the door open to the work of the Holy Spirit in your life and in theirs? Pray for ways you can leave a door open to the possible restoration.

IT'S NOT YOUR JOB TO RESCUE OTHER PEOPLE

One of my favorite cousins lives in South Africa. She has been like a surrogate mom to me over the years and her husband is a doctor. Several years ago he suffered an accidental needle prick. It comes with the territory in the medical field. But for a long, terrible while he didn't know if he had been infected with a virus or not.

It was a hard load to live under.

They didn't tell their kids the source of their worry, but children internalize their parents' anxiety. And their small frames and hearts got heavier and more stooped under the weight of the worry they could feel in their house. They kept trying to carry it with their small hands, and positive attitudes, and big eyes, wanting to ask questions they were afraid to hear answers to. They could tell their parents were struggling with an unspoken fear, and the littles kept breathing in that air of anxiety until it became part of their own DNA, and they adopted that unspoken worry like it was their own. And of course, it almost crushed their tiny frames.

So my cousin and her husband intervened. One night after supper they lined up all three children (at the time aged 6 and under). A game of pretend was initiated and each kid was given their school backpack to put on. Their parents followed them around the house and yard slowly, methodically adding rocks to the backpacks.

Big, solid, heavy rocks. They kept filling the backpacks with those rocks.

At first, the children enjoyed the challenge. They could do it. They could still run and play with the heavy packs. But rock after rock had them slowing down until all three of them were at a standstill and the game had lost its fun.

"We can't do this, Dad," said their oldest daughter.
"Why? Why can't you?" her father pushed back.
"Because they're too heavy. We're just kids; they're too heavy for us."

Tired, worried eyes looked out from scrunched up faces at their parents. And the parents? They did what parents do. They began unpacking their children's anxieties.

They acknowledged the ominous dread that had entered the house and that the kids had taken to carrying upon themselves. They slowly and clearly explained that this worry was not a weight designed for children. That it was too heavy for them. That managing it, or carrying it, or even trying to balance it was not up to them. They were not required to bear their parents' fears.

And with that they reached into the backpacks that had been dragging down three sets of small shoulders and began to unpack them. They removed each of those heavy, solid rocks and hurled them into the back garden. The children got in on the spirit of the thing. Satchel straps slipped off small arms, and eager hands grabbed at ugly burdens and threw them far away until those kids were free of the baggage that never belonged to them in the first place.

Sometimes friendship can feel like that. Sometimes, without even realizing we're doing it, we start accumulating the heavy rocks and sharp pieces of broken glass that our friends have been carrying, and we put them into our own backpacks. We stuff ourselves full of our friends' hurts and frustrations and heavy, difficult stories, and then we wonder why it's so hard to keep walking forward.

> Think of a friendship where you collected and carried the broken rocks and sharp glass pieces that didn't really belong to you. Describe what that looked and felt like.

Here's where it gets tricky. As Christians we're taught that it's a good thing to be willing to, "Bear one another's burdens, and so fulfill the law of Christ" (Gal. 6:2, ESV). But, if we aren't careful, that can guilt us into putting up with a lot of behavior that is harmful to us. Because being willing to "bear one another's burdens" is not the same as being willing to bear one another's dysfunction, rage, inappropriate behavior, manipulation, passive aggression, cruelty, control, and a whole host of other traits that we can inhale like secondhand smoke in some friendships without even being aware of it.

But when we spend some time with those first verses in Galatians chapter 6, we discover that the challenge to "bear one another's burdens" is in fact a call to hold one another accountable for our "moral burdens or weaknesses."[1] It is not an excuse to enable those behaviors. See for yourself, what does verse 1 say?

Rewrite Galatians 6:1 in your own words.

The Greek word for the verb "restore" used in verse 1 is used in other places in the New Testament to talk about "mending nets … and bringing factions together."[2] This is about assistance, not taking on others' problems as our own. This is about friendship motivated by faithfulness, not manipulated by guilt.

Let's look at the instructions for healthy relationships in Galatians 6:1-5. I think they can be summed up in three strong calls to action:

- Verse 1: Mend
- Verses 2: Carry.
- Verses 3-5: Attend.

Let's unpack that a bit.

> Brothers and sisters, if someone is overtaken in any wrongdoing, you who are spiritual, restore such a person with a gentle spirit, watching out for yourselves so that you also won't be tempted. Carry one another's burdens; in this way you will fulfill the law of Christ. For if anyone considers himself to be something when he is nothing, he deceives himself. Let each person examine his own work, and then he can take pride in himself alone, and not compare himself with someone else. For each person will have to carry his own load.
> —GALATIANS 6:1-5

VERSE 1: MEND

The challenge is to restore or mend a friend so she finds her way back toward better choices—back toward Christ.

Highlight the words in verse 1 that illustrate this challenge.

Now, explain what that might look like in real life for you and your friends.

VERSE 2: CARRY

The second challenge is to carry a friend's burdens—those burdens that create a crushing "physical, emotional, or spiritual load."[3]

Highlight the words in verse 2 that illustrate that challenge.

Now, note how the charge to "mend a friend" comes before the charge to "carry one another's burdens." Why do you think this is important?

This order is important because it helps us keep our obligations straight. Instead of being guilted into making excuses for a friend's bad behavior, we're called to first be an agent of change in her life and to help mend bad behavior before we offer broad and sympathetic shoulders as she works her way out from under that burden. We are called to be agents of change. We are not called to enable bad behavior. And we are definitely not called to adopt their bad behavior as our own. Remember what the second part of verse 1 said.

VERSES 3-5: ATTEND

The challenge in these verses is to attend to your own load, without comparing, condescending, or controlling.

Highlight the words in verses 3-5 that illustrate that challenge.

Note, the Greek word used here for "load" is not the same word used in verse 2 for "burdens." Instead, in this verse the word means the *cargo* or *capacity* that we've been assigned by the Lord.[4] While mending and attending to our friends, we can't become distracted from the responsibility of carrying our own loads—the specific callings, challenges, or tests that Christ has entrusted to us. We don't trade one in for the other. Instead, we remain faithful to both.

Why do these three challenges (and the order they appear) to mend, carry, and attend matter so much?

I think they matter because we're not always good at getting the order or the actions right. As Christian girls, I think we are particularly susceptible to the "disease of politeness." It can be deadly. It can force us to make excuses instead of take action. Even when we're deep in a relationship that's starting to throttle us because we've exchanged the loads God has entrusted us with for the baggage friends have guilted us with.

In their book, *Safe People*, Henry Cloud and John Townsend unpack what hopeful creatures we humans are and how it's that very optimism that can keep us making excuses or hoping for change. And instead of helping mend, we've started to bend to accommodate the behaviors of friends long past the point of healthy interactions:

> Humans are incredible optimists when it comes to destructive relationships. For some reason we think that a person who is hurtful, irresponsible, out of control, abusive, or dishonest is going to change if we just love them correctly or more or enough. We think that if we just let them know about their mistakes, or cry the blues, or get angry, that they will change. … In this scenario we use hope to defend ourselves against facing the truth about someone we love. We do not want to go through the sadness of realizing that they probably are not going to change. We don't want to accept the reality about who they are. So, we hope.[5]

So what then? What if we have tried all three steps—mending, carrying, and attending—and nothing has changed? How do we love well without being dragged under by the weight of a friendship that's become too heavy and too unhealthy to keep carrying? How do we figure out when to keep trying and when it might be beyond our ability to fix things?

We'll unpack those answers over the next two days. For today, it's important to simply make sure we understand what God has required of us and to keep in mind that it's not our job to rescue other people, it's our job to love them. It's Jesus' job to rescue them.

Are you carrying around someone else's broken bits and pieces in your backpack? Has it started to feel too heavy? Is it starting to cause you resentment, bitterness, or panic?

Friendship Challenge

Be really honest. List the things you think you might have taken on that were never yours to carry in the first place.

Now, identify your own mend, carry, attend journey. Chart it so you know where you currently are in relation to that friendship.

FEAR GOD NOT PEOPLE

If ever there was a handbook on how to negotiate difficult relationships and create fresh starts, it's the Bible: "The chief theme of the entire Bible is reconciliation of unsafe relationships."[6] First, between us and God. And second between us and the other people God has created. All throughout Scripture we see how God is relentless in His quest to remake us in His own image, often through our relationships with other people. Even the challenging relationships. Sometimes especially through those.

God is in the business of doing what according to Revelation 21:5?

This is what God modeled in His own relationships. He didn't give up on the difficult, frustrating ones. Instead, He facilitated healing. We see Him do this with Adam and Eve, Cain, Noah, Moses, Joshua, Rahab, David, Ruth, Peter, Paul, and on and on throughout history to the bickering disciples, the early church, and all the way up to you, and me, and that girl at school who makes you grind your teeth in irritation. God wants wholeness. God wants health. He wants people to experience eternal, unbroken relationships with Him. Obviously, things didn't quite end up like that:

> People turned toward self-centeredness and away from God and his ways. And God was faced with the same dilemma that we are faced with in our relationships in a fallen world: Do I keep them, or do I move on?[7]

Every time I bump into another real time, real life example that God understands my life from the inside out, I'm surprised all over again. That He understands my tender scabs where friendships have cut and where I haven't been able to put things back together again. I'm amazed that the God of the universe and I share the same aching cry that sometimes comes out as a whimper and sometimes as a gut cry of confusion, "I have been *hurt*" (Ezek. 6:9, NASB; emphasis mine). Another translation says, "I was *crushed* by their promiscuous hearts that turned away from me" (CSB; emphasis mine).

God gets it. From the inside out He knows what a betrayal by a friend feels like. And His pain can be heard loudly from the pages of both the Old and the

New Testaments. If He's our role model in His hurt, then He can also be trusted as our role model in how to respond. And it's not what you might think. It's not a quick kick to the curb. No, instead God lives up to His own Word and His character.

READ 1 CORINTHIANS 13:4-7.

Jot down God's defining character traits listed in these verses.

Nothing will require us to put these into practice like relationships with other people. Indeed, you wouldn't need this list if you were the only human being on the planet. This is a checklist for how to thrive alongside other human beings. Drs. Cloud and Townsend conclude from this list what God's consistent response to hurt has been throughout Scripture, down through history, and into our own lives today:

WE FIND THAT GOD

1. Starts from a loved position,
2. acts righteously,
3. uses the community to transform us,
4. accepts reality and forgives us,
5. gives change a chance, and
6. is long-suffering.[8]

This list is not what I want to hear when I'm worn down by a difficult relationship. Instead, when I've done all that I believe I can, I have been known to tell God, "Well, I'm done." As I metaphorically dust off my hands and pat myself on the back for giving it such a good go. And I believe it. I'm done being patient, and done trying to stand in her shoes, and done trying to keep my heart open, and done keeping my passive aggression in check, and done with second, third, fourth chances.

And I believe I'm justified in feeling that way because just look, God! Look at all my hard work. Look at how I've cried and wrestled and felt like crap and gone back and tried again. And look where we *still* are. Obviously this has to be the end, yes? I mean, at some point we run out of trying. We run out of do-overs. We run out of interest, or patience, or conversations. At some point, surely, we both just get to be done.

But God, I have found, is stubborn. And He has stubbornly insisted in my life that there is no *done* when it comes to sacrificial love. There is only "more." This has been a shocking revelation to me—shocking and, frankly, unwelcome—to discover that more would be expected of me. More listening. More changing. More bending. More willingness to be open. More awkward and more choosing to stay instead of cutting loose and quitting. God has kept me in some relationships way past what I would have considered to be the finish line.

But He hasn't left me there alone. He's always been intimately involved and insanely patient with me. And it has changed me. That's the kicker. It has changed me when I thought it was about changing the other person. It has taken apart all my assumptions about love and kindness and patience and that old-school word, *long-suffering,* and put them back together again in a picture that demonstrates how eternal God's patience is with me. With all of us.

> Look up the definition of *long-suffering* and write it out in your own words.

I have found Him rabid in His ability to out-wait our selfishness, our stubbornness, our insistence on doing things our own way. He has walked me down the winding corridors of "more" miles and miles further than I ever would have thought my legs or my heart could take. There will be some relationships that are so poisoned and bitter that we need to stop letting them feed us; we need to cut the ties, and we need to walk away so that we can live. So that both of us can live. So that we can thrive in our individual lanes and keep running hard for the kingdom. And we'll talk more about those tomorrow.

But there are other friendships that are an assignment straight from Jesus Himself—that He's using to get up in your business and teach you some things about yourself. Some friendships where He's asking you to actually *be* His patience and grace and compassion personified in actual arms and time and conversations. Friendships where there isn't a shortcut to cutting out the tension that seems to have grown up out of nowhere between you. Being human comes with other human beings so if we stop, drop, and cut them off any time we're offended, annoyed, frustrated, or unable to make sense of the current state of the friendship, we will soon find ourselves friendless and alone.

Yesterday, I sat down at my desk and made a list of the things I've lost because of friendships. Because of friends who have challenged me, pushed me out of my comfort zone, and forced me to look up from the solar system of my own creation where I've so regularly assumed I was the sun. The truth of it is that those friendships, the ones that have rubbed me raw as they've reminded me that I am not the center of the universe, have given me the gift of *subtraction*. We're so one-track minded when it comes to friendship; so programmed to look for what's in it for, that sometimes we forget the best thing we can get out of a friendship might be one of the things we have lost because of it.

My most difficult friendships have cost me. The love and patience they've required have cost me huge chunks of my pride. I've lost parts of my arrogance along the way and my inability to see the world from someone else's perspective. I've lost my unwillingness to compromise, and I've had to give up my stubborn refusal to apologize.

Some friendships are like a punching bag. And sometimes that is what our hearts require. Our puffed up, stubborn, arrogant hearts sometimes need the pounding, tenderizing mercy of a God who wants us to be malleable, capable of profound compassion, and quick to give someone else the benefit of the doubt. Being willing to let God work in me and through me for the sake of healing what was once a deeply unhealthy friendship has been nothing short of miraculous.

But it's required a focus on Him instead of my default of stewing and obsessing about how I'm being treated by a friend. It has required paying attention to what God wants, not what my friend or I want. It has required not letting my feelings be the boss of me. Instead, it's been about recognizing that if a friendship has any hope of surviving, I need to let the Holy Spirit be the boss of me. Because where we go for wisdom in these frustrating friendship moments is essential.

My own gut, or temper, or self-pity are terrible places to look for wisdom.

LET'S READ PROVERBS 9:10 AND PSALM 111:10.

In both of these passages, what is described as the beginning or the foundation of wisdom?

Jesus was constantly loving beyond the borders of what we can ever begin to imagine. His love was lavish, unafraid, and extravagant. He opened His heart and His life to the people who loved Him back as well as to those who spit in His face. That kind of love will wrench you. It will wring you out. It will require more of you than you thought possible. But it will drive you deep into Jesus' side until His feelings become your feelings and together you might just find a miracle—the dry bones of a dead friendship coming back to life.

In Oswald Chambers' words, "It is impossible to exhaust God's love, and it is impossible to exhaust my love if it flows from the Spirit of God within me."[9] We can always borrow God's feelings for our friends when we're struggling with our own. He promises to pour Himself out into us and then through us and the only thing we have to do is bring willingness to the equation. We have to be willing to receive His patience, kindness, long-suffering nature, and love, and then be willing to pass it on to our friends.

I like to think, I need to believe, that those rough edges of my younger self are slowly being sanded away by friends who've lived alongside me and rubbed off on me with their own generous grace where none was deserved. So that when those bumpy days arrive and you start to doubt your friends and it becomes hard to keep believing the best about them, I remember that sometimes the best work God does inside our souls is the most uncomfortable.

So on those days, on the days I am struggling to feel love, grace, compassion, or patience toward other humans, I ask God if I can borrow His feelings. If can swap all my frustration for a slice of His worldview and a chunk of His feelings toward my fellow womankind. This is God who has loved them deeper and longer and who knows their rough edges and hurt insides better than we ever will. And this is the God who generously pours out His love and who never runs out and who is defined by compassion and speaks in grace and walked the walk all the way to the cross and down into the dark tomb and out into the light again. With access to that kind of love, my own tired heart can be resurrected and keep opening up to keep loving while buried deeply and safely inside the shield of His own.

> "For it is God who is working in you both to will [feel/want] and to work [act] according to his good purpose." —PHILIPPIANS 2:13

God will supply you with the feelings and He will do the work—in you and through you and for you—so that you can be a blessing to the girls around you instead of letting Satan explode a relationship that Jesus is trying to put back together.

Friendship Challenge

What are the things that you've lost because of friendships? The things you needed to lose? Spend some time thinking back on challenging friendships that have helped grow you up.

_____

_____

_____

_____

_____

Now, when you think about challenging friendships, does someone specific come to mind? Is there a girl who is rubbing you the wrong way? Instead of giving into your irritation with her, let's spend some time today asking God what He might be trying to teach you through that friendship. What does He want you to lose to make room for more of Him? Pray, open your heart, and then write down what comes to mind.

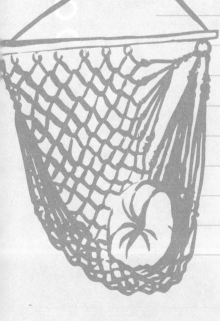

_____

_____

_____

_____

_____

_____

_____

DAY 3

WALK AWAY WISELY

The reality of friendship is that we live in a broken world. A world broken by sin. And we feel the consequences of that daily. We serve a King who has given His life to redeem this broken world and to put it back together. He is at work in the world building His kingdom and making stained glass art out of all the sharp and shattered bits and pieces of our lives. But in the midst of that process He has been up front and told us that we will have trouble in this world (John 16:33). This world will break our hearts the way it broke His. And while He has overcome the world, if we follow in His footsteps, we will share in His scars.

Jesus left this world with scars on His hands, feet, and side, and I'm certain they crisscrossed deep, painful grooves into His heart. So if your own heart aches, then know you are not alone. You are living the legacy of the God who came to show us the way. The God who rode into Jerusalem weeping for the people and the city who would betray Him and themselves. But that didn't slow Him down or stop Him from coming to them, from coming to us.

So when a friendship has broken into bits and pieces too painful for us to keep carrying, then in my experience we can offer them back to Jesus. Leaning deep into Jesus' sacrificial love will walk you much deeper and longer into opening your heart up to love people you never thought you could love until the friendship is either healed or you recognize that it's beyond your ability to raise from the dead; that you can't carry that burden anymore.

Then, friend, I believe that Jesus will lift the burden off you. But here's what makes Him the very definition of love, He won't discard that friend. No, I believe He will take the burden onto His own shoulders and into His own heart—the place where it has lived all along—and He will keep carrying it Himself. He will free you to walk alongside Him as He carries all that hurt and pain all the way with Him up onto the cross and down into the grave and back out into the light again. While darkness might try to blot out a friendship, Jesus is the light of the world.

In him was life, and that life was the light of men. That light shines in the darkness, and yet the darkness did not overcome it. —JOHN 1:4-5

What do these verses say about the attempt by darkness to blot out Christ's light?

It is not for us to judge the hearts of our friends. It's for us to keep following Jesus. And in some friendships that will mean following Him as He walks us away from a friend. Those relationships riddled with so much hurt and so many unhealthy habits that, instead of growing us both toward God, grew us away—like poison ivy that would choke the life out of the trees it wrap itself around and sting anyone who tries to remove it.

In order to be agents of peace, of long-suffering, of long walks with a God who doesn't turn His back on a relationship, we need to be healthy ourselves. Every time a relationship has been more toxic than I could possibly transform, I was either too young, or too vulnerable, or too unqualified to be able to make anything healthy out of that environment. Some wounds need professional, tender counseling from those qualified to speak objectively into a raw and hurting person. In those cases, God has given me the protection of being able to grant forgiveness while simultaneously opening an exit for me to leave so there was a still a chance to heal separately. Forgiveness does not negate consequence, and change has to be chosen—it can't be forced.

I remember the afternoon God released me from a friendship I couldn't seem to save. I was driving our old, red pickup truck at the end of a hot, sticky day. The windows were down because the air conditioning wasn't working. I was driving to pick up burgers and fries for dinner. As usual I was twisting my mind into knots trying to make sense of how to keep walking forward in a friendship that seemed to keep moving backward. I was so tired, but I was more determined than I'd ever been to love far beyond my borders. To love in a way that didn't make sense to me. To love even when I didn't understand if anything good was coming out of that loving.

As I passed a small white chapel and pulled into the fast food parking lot, I felt a weight shift off my heart. It seemed that the Holy Spirit had said two words to me: "You're done." Just like that. The task He'd sent me was over. I won't know till I meet God face to face if I walked as far and true and deeply into the call of love He'd set before me as He wanted me to or not. I won't know if my attempt came close to what He was asking of me. But today, I know that I no longer carry that load. Instead He's taken it onto His wide, trustworthy shoulders and let me walk out from under the burden.

> Describe a time when you felt released from a situation like mine—a friendship that you were no longer required to try to fix.

But we release those burdens and walk away from those friendships slowly; without slamming and bolting the door behind us. Because we believe in a God who raises hopeless, dead bones back to life. And with my hope firmly placed in Him, I want that door unlocked so that friendship has a chance for resurrection. But until then I know I can trust Him with it. Because our God of *shalom* doesn't just want wholeness. He is wholeness. He is "the way, the truth, and the life" (John 14:6), moving all of humanity toward right relationship with Him and with each other *through* Him.

I've heard versions of this same story told over plates of pizza and across a farmhouse table over shared chips and salsa. One friend said she thought it had been good-bye. She thought there wouldn't be room for restoration, but she never stopped praying. Four years later the shut door of a dear friendship creaked its way back open again.

Another wise woman told the story of 15 years spent interceding for a brutally difficult relationship at work. Transfer or resignation would have been her preference, but God kept her praying and at times begging Him for health, for life, and for hope in this broken relationship. "Those are the kinds of prayers," she told me, "that God loves to answer." Fifteen years later and the evening she told us the story she'd just come home from the funeral of her colleague's son. A funeral she still couldn't believe she'd been invited to attend—with the woman she's since held in her arms as they wept together. The woman who spent years refusing to talk to her.

Jesus and Paul both taught that, sometimes we have to leave someone; that some relationships have to end.[10]

> Write down the relationship that ended in each of these passages and why.
> Matthew 18:15-17   Titus 3:10

There are also examples of relationships being restored in the stories that the Bible preserved for us.

Read how Paul and Barnabas disagreed over John Mark, but Paul later took Mark with him:

> After some time had passed, Paul said to Barnabas, "Let's go back and visit the brothers and sisters in every town where we have preached the word of the Lord and see how they're doing." Barnabas wanted to take along John Mark. But Paul insisted that they should not take along this man who had deserted them in Pamphylia and had not gone on with them to the work. They had such a sharp disagreement that they parted company, and Barnabas took Mark with him and sailed off to Cyprus. But Paul chose Silas and departed, after being commended by the brothers and sisters to the grace of the Lord. —ACTS 15:36-40

Why didn't Paul want to take Mark with them?

What kind of disagreement did Paul and Barnabas have?

> Aristarchus, my fellow prisoner, sends you greetings, as does Mark, Barnabas's cousin (concerning whom you have received instructions: if he comes to you, welcome him). —COLOSSIANS 4:10

What was Mark's relationship to Barnabas?

What sentence tells us Mark was with Paul?

How did Paul say that the church in Colossae should treat Mark?

While we sometimes have to separate ourselves from a friend, we hope that this separation isn't forever. Part of what Jesus' brother, James, describes as the "hard work of getting along" (Jas. 3:18, MSG) in community includes being willing to address inappropriate behavior and set appropriate boundaries with consequences.

I have learned that forgiveness doesn't require friendship in order to be genuine. Forgiveness does not equal allowing unsafe people into our safe, inner circles. Drs. Cloud and Townsend describe boundaries this way:

> Boundaries are our spiritual and emotional "property lines." They tell us where we end, and where others begin. They help to keep good things in us, and bad things out. We take responsibility for what is ours, and not for what isn't. When we are clearly defined, we can carry our own loads, and we know when it's appropriate to help others with their burdens (Gal. 6:1–5).[11]

Drawing safe boundary lines doesn't make you selfish, unchristian, or impolite. It makes you wise. And it puts your hope in the right place—in the Christ who can actually transform and who won't disappoint instead of in our friends who can't help but fail us, because like us, they're human and flawed (Rom. 5:5). Safe boundary lines and housing your hope in the right place will make you all the more capable of being a girl who is a safe place for her friends to unload their heavy burdens and trust that they will find encouragement in the shade of your friendship without codependency or guilt.

Whether we like it or not, we all haul some kind of baggage with us into our future friendships. And we all need to be reminded that we're not responsible for the luggage that other girls will bring with them. But that we will be impacted by it and should be ready for when those suitcases of junk inevitably explode at inconvenient times when all you thought you were doing was making plans for lunch. And instead you end up down a dark and twisting conversation you never expected.

Take a minute to reflect on the last few paragraphs. When have you needed to put boundaries in place for the sake of yourself or your friendship?

Jesus-type friendship is about taking His Word literally when it says, "If it is possible, as far as it depends on you, live at peace with everyone" (Rom. 12:18, NIV). We won't know if it is possible to live at peace with others, until we have tried everything to live at peace with them.[12] If we have followed in Christ's footsteps and behaved in a way that honors our friend and our Savior. That checklist for living at peace with everyone, as far as it depends on you, might look something like this:

- ☐ **START FROM A LOVED POSITION.** I will approach this relationship from the security of my identity in Christ, rejecting codependency, and believing that in Christ I am loved, chosen, and cherished (John 3:16).

- ☐ **ACT RIGHTEOUSLY.** I take responsibility for how my own behavior may have impacted the friendship. I will work to change, ask forgiveness where necessary, and move toward health (Matt. 7:1-5). I am not simply returning "evil for evil" (Rom. 12:17).

- ☐ **RELY ON COMMUNITY. I WON'T JUST TRUST MY OWN OPINION.** I will be honest with friends who know us both, ask for their advice, and be open to learn and change and grow from it (Prov. 11:14).

- ☐ **ACCEPT REALITY AND FORGIVE.** I won't try to twist my friend into my own image. I have accepted her as she is, uniquely created in God's image. And where she has hurt me, I have not held a grudge. I can honestly say that I have freely forgiven her as Christ forgave me (Eph. 4:32).

- ☐ **GIVE CHANGE A CHANCE.** I won't quit when the friendship gets tough. I will stay. I will love and forgive. I will let God change me where I need it. And I am open to seeing the friendship grow and change (Matt. 18:21-22).

- ☐ **PRACTICE PATIENCE.** I will not give up on this friendship easily. When God has asked me to, I will go the extra mile with my whole heart (Ex. 34:6-7).[13]

Go back and read through the list above. Check any areas you are working through in your own current friendships.

When we have faithfully and honestly done these things, then we can know that we are girls who are safe places for friendship. We are girls undaunted by the hard or heavy stories our friends bring with them into our friendships. But we are also girls who can be released from the false guilt we so often feel at the thought of walking away from an unhealthy friendship—a friendship that as far as it is possible, *as far as it depends on you*, you haven't been able to fix.

Giving ourselves permission to forgive the hurt of a friendship and still walk away from it is a necessary life skill. *But emphasis on the walk*. This isn't about running away from friends, quitting friendships, or ruthlessly cutting inconvenient friends out of your life. This is about becoming safe people for the sake of ourselves and our friends. And sometimes that requires distance.

Leaving a friendship will come with sadness. Jesus was called a "man of sorrows" (Isa. 53:3, ESV), and those of us who want to follow Him won't be immune from His grief. When we walk away from a destructive relationship, there's a loss and sadness. If we do not face the loss, and the sadness with it, we can find ourselves going back to the same relationship or another destructive one like it.[14]

We worship a God who is defined by His passion to make "everything new" (Rev. 21:5), and Christ makes all things new (2 Cor. 5:17)—even (and maybe especially) friendships between His daughters.

In the meantime, He invites us to wield the power of praise. Let's end our time together by reading the staggering story of King Jehoshaphat and how he overcame terrible odds by the power of praising the Lord.

READ 2 CHRONICLES 20:14-26.

The valley where God handed them the victory was named the Valley of Berakah. Why? What does that mean according to verse 26?

In the face of lost friendships and scarred hearts, there might be nothing as unexpected or as powerful as refusing to sink under the sea of false guilt or sadness but instead throwing out our arms as we lean into a life praising the God who is the giver of all good gifts, especially the gift of friendship. This moment right now that aches, this moment that comes with scars, it might be the moment you remember as your Valley of Praise.

So, sisters, stand firm, keep focused on what God has asked you to do, and wield the power of praise over every aspect of your friendships. Especially today.

Friendship Challenge

READ JAMES 3:17-18. My favorite version is in The Message.

Real wisdom, God's wisdom, begins with a holy life and is characterized by getting along with others. It is gentle and reasonable, overflowing with mercy and blessings, not hot one day and cold the next, not two-faced. You can develop a healthy, robust community that lives right with God and enjoy its results *only* if you do the hard work of getting along with each other, treating each other with dignity and honor.
—JAMES 3:17-18

Jot down each aspect of healthy friendship highlighted by this passage.

_____

_____

Now, ask yourself three final questions:

1. Am I honestly doing the hard work of getting along with my friends? How?

2. If not, what should I start doing differently? Or if so, what can I practice doing better? Be very specific in your answers. Here is your chance to challenge yourself and to go deeper in your friendships.

3. Have I embraced the power of praise in my life? Let's end our time together by writing down a prayer of praise to the God who is the very definition of friendship. Let's thank Him for the gift of His friendship, the example of His friendship, and the challenge of His friendship. Amen and amen.

_____

_____

_____

FRIENDSHIP isn't something we passively RECEIVE. FRIENDSHIP is something we actively DO.

#WSYAS

FRIENDSHIP TAKES ACTION

"Which of these three do you think proved to be a neighbor to the man who fell into the hands of the robbers?"
"The one who showed mercy to him," he said.
Then Jesus told him, "Go and do the same."

LUKE 10:36-37

Friendship takes action

It's time to dare to go first—be the friend you want to have. No more repeating the pattern of waiting on friendship to happen spontaneously and being resentful when it doesn't. Friendship requires your active initiation and participation.

Describe a time when you "dared to go first."

READ LUKE 10:25-37.

The parable of the good Samaritan isn't about *identifying* your neighbor; it's about *being* a neighbor. In essence, it's about being the kind of friend you wish you had. The story doesn't identify who you are supposed to love; it's about taking the initiative to love someone in completely unexpected ways when it is not even required.

Giving love when it was not expected defined Jesus' entire ministry. He came to be a neighbor to us, and that is the challenge that He gives back to us. Go and be a neighbor, take the action—be the first.

What does this look like in your life? How can you be a neighbor, invite people in, and create opportunities for friendship?

READ MARK 2:1-12.

The friends of the paralyzed man were willing to go to great lengths to help him. This kind of friendship requires both action (dismantling a roof so you can lower your friend down to Jesus) and a willingness to receive (like the paralyzed man did). It must have required a unique humility to accept such bold help from friends. Both action and humility come with a continual breaking down of pride and exercising the boldness to ask and the grace to receive. Are we willing to initiate and receive that kind of friendship—refusing to simply say, "I'm fine"? It takes vulnerability to allow friends to surround us and help us to stand.

How can being on the receiving end of friendship sometimes be difficult for us?

How has God used other people to bring change or transformation in your life?

Friends can surprise us in the care they have for us, in the lengths they are willing to go to help us stand. Afterward, the world witnesses the glory of God in that friendship and in that love.

How have you seen friendship do the work of the body of Christ?

Consider the story of the good Samaritan again. Imagine yourself as the person beaten and left on the ground. You accept help from a person you have been told is not your friend and not your neighbor. The person you have been warned against is now the person coming to you and showing you love. We don't get to choose the girls that God will place in our lives, but we can choose to love them well.

How do you see Christ's love for us through your friendships with others?

Entering into a friendship with the people God places in front of you puts you in a place of humility. When we open ourselves to the friends God has placed in our lives, God makes things happen. God changes people through other people. We were all created for community and we need friendship.

Describe how you have seen the need for friendship embedded into our spiritual DNA.

We always have a choice—either to move closer to friends or move farther away. Jesus shows us who He is through those relationships with other people. Don't miss out on the opportunity to see Him in those moments. Scripture invites us to pursue Christ and to pursue friendship with the people He's created.

Think about all you've learned about friendships over the last six weeks. Go back through each week, and highlight one thing that stood out to you, made a difference in your relationships, or that you'd like to apply to your friendships now. Ask God to continue to work in you, in your relationships, and through your relationships.

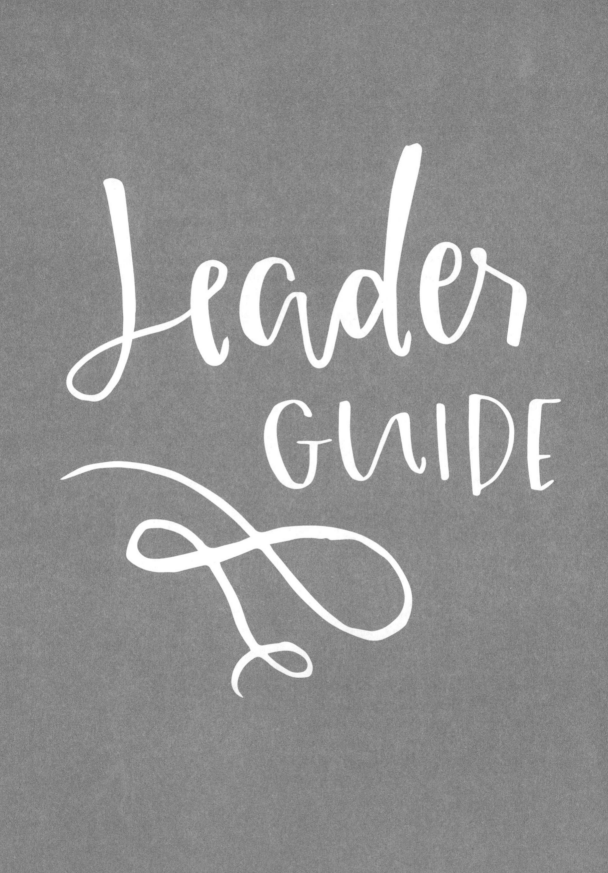

WEEK 1

GET STARTED (OPTIONAL)

- Begin this first week with an activity to break the ice and get the girls interacting. Today will include a lot of honest sharing, so try to help girls feel comfortable and ready to open up.

- Before your group meets, create a list of famous best friends. Some examples include Buzz and Woody, Justin Timberlake and Jimmy Fallon, and Amy Poehler and Tina Fey. Place the girls in groups of two and give each pair the names of two celebrity best friends. Instruct girls to imitate their celebrity friends, while the rest of the group tries to guess the famous best friends.

MAKE IT PERSONAL

- Be willing to go first for your girls. They need an example of how to be "not fine." Be vulnerable by talking about your "not fine" day, then allow girls a chance to discuss and share their own honest moments.

- Friendship is challenging, and it is easy to block chances for community to grow by putting up fences and hiding behind excuses. Girls might think they have too much homework or that they don't have anything in common with the new girl. Encourage them to stop hiding behind the easy answers and too busy excuses. Take every opportunity to let friendship grow and listen to the joys and sorrows of friends.

- Growing friendship takes diligent work and purposeful attention. Make sure students understand that being a best friend will look different in every relationship, because we are all different.

BEFORE YOU GO

- Remind girls to work through the homework days on their own.

- Close by praying for your group. Pray specifically over the girls and for meaningful friendships that can create community. Pray that girls will seek friendship and be intentional in their relationships.

WEEK 2

GET STARTED (OPTIONAL)

- Provide each girl with a piece of paper and a pen. Explain that, in each scenario, girls must choose who they would call for help.

  1. You just received a breakup text. Who do you talk to?

  2. You have to make a big decision. Who gives the best advice?

  3. You've had a big fight with your parents. Who will understand?

  4. You're very sick and need someone to pray with. Who will comfort and pray with you?

  5. A girl you thought was a friend is spreading rumors. Who can advise and counsel you?

- Ask girls how they chose their people. Each person they choose will be someone they trust with the biggest moments of their lives. Someone they are willing to show the vulnerable places.

MAKE IT PERSONAL

- We are a culture that hides behind Instagram perfect lives. We are unwilling to show even our closest friends the mess that lies behind our perfect pictures. Don't let girls stop short by sharing only on the surface level. Dig deeper and reveal the vulnerable pieces to create stronger friendships and community.

- Share with the group about a friend the Lord placed in your life. How was she there for you at just the right moment?

- Were you ever surprised by your friends? Share a story of when God surprised you with a friendship that you never expected.

BEFORE YOU GO

- Remind girls to finish the homework days on their own.

- Close by praying for your group. Thank God for the growing friendships among your group and for the opportunity to create a stronger community. Pray that girls will continue to be vulnerable with each other and with God. Pray specifically for any prayer requests and for girls who shared hurts or broken relationships in need of healing.

WEEK 3

GET STARTED (OPTIONAL)

- Ask girls whether they are more likely to work together as a team or against each other as competitors in the following situations.

  1. Playing a game of volleyball with friends

  2. Playing on a varsity sports team

  3. Working on a group project for school

  4. Playing a board game

  5. Discussing an issue in class

  6. Making family decisions

MAKE IT PERSONAL

- We all hear the voice of comparison in our heads, and it can be difficult to silence that voice. Share a personal story with the group about a time when you were fighting feelings of competition and still risked a friendship.

- Rocky relationships and distant friendships are exactly what Satan wants. He wants to see only competition and not encouragement or opportunities for shared joy. Help girls think of ways that they can purposefully encourage one another.

- Being supportive and encouraging is especially difficult when facing challenges. How can girls still be supportive when it's another girl who ran faster, or scored higher, or finished first? It is difficult to encourage friends and share in their joy when we are not in the same place of happiness. Take some time with your group to acknowledge this struggle and address some ways to remain encouraging even when we don't feel like it.

BEFORE YOU GO

- Remind girls to finish the homework days on their own.

- Close by praying for your group. Pray specifically for the girls in group today and for the growing friendships you see there. Pray that girls will have hearts that encourage community and joy, not competition and envy. Pray that girls will be God-centered and that He will replace their selfish hearts with a pure and giving heart like His.

WEEK 4

GET STARTED (OPTIONAL)

- Choose two girls to sit on the floor back to back. Instruct the girls to stand up without using their hands. Once two girls are able to stand, try with three sitting with their backs together on the ground. Keep adding students until your entire group is trying to stand together.

MAKE IT PERSONAL

- The cool kids. No matter how old we get, we can always look around and spot the cool kids. But this isn't actually true—there are no cool kids and that perception could be blocking us from building lasting friendships. Make this personal for girls by sharing a story about how you did not let the "cool kid" status stop you or by sharing about a missed opportunity when you were held back by fear of an awkward encounter.

- Another way girls may be missing opportunities is by watching over their shoulders or waiting for a better offer to come along. It's very common for all of us to commit to time with friends and then back out at the last minute. Maybe you got a better offer from another person and decided to meet another friend instead. Or maybe you just decided to stay at home. Either way, we are not allowing our yeses to mean yes, and our noes to mean no. Talk with your girls about being intentional with their time. Don't commit to something unless you actually plan to attend, and if you say yes, then it means yes.

BEFORE YOU GO

- Remind girls to finish the homework days on their own.

- Close by praying for your group. Pray this week for girls to be intentional with their time. Pray that girls will not worry over the cool kids or be stopped by insecurities. Ask God to give each girl the heart of a servant that is willing to serve just as Jesus showed us.

WEEK 5

- Before you begin your study this week, write out the names of famous pairs on separate name tags. For example, include the words *peanut butter* on one tag and *jelly* on another, or *Patrick* on one and *SpongeBob* on another. As girls arrive, place a tag on their backs where they cannot read their own tags. Tell girls not to reveal what is on each other's tags. Once everyone has arrived, instruct girls to move around the room and find the match to the name on their backs. They may use only yes or no questions to figure out what is written on their tags and who is their match. Once each pair has been matched, ask girls to sit with their "matches" during group time and discuss answers together when it's time to share personal stories.

MAKE IT PERSONAL

- This week's study is a difficult one—it will require a lot of truthful talk and willingness to be vulnerable. Many girls may have hurting hearts, but encourage them that it takes acknowledging that hurt in order to find forgiveness and, ultimately, healing.

- Share with your group about a time when you have been deeply hurt by a friend. How did you practice forgiveness in that situation? How were you able to move past the hurt and form new friendships?

BEFORE YOU GO

- Remind girls to finish the homework days on their own.

- Close by praying for your group. Pray specifically for any hurts that were shared during group. Ask God to help girls forgive past hurts and move forward into healing, following in Jesus' footsteps.

- Be deliberate in your time this week and follow up with girls who need prayers for healing.

WEEK 6

GET STARTED (OPTIONAL)

- Provide blank cards for each girl in your group. Before the girls arrive, place a card and a pen on each seat. Ask girls to choose a seat and write their names on the envelope for the card. After everyone has arrived, ask girls to mix it up and choose a new seat (not the one directly beside them). Once they are in new seats, instruct girls to write an encouraging note to the girl whose name is on the envelope. After the girls have finished writing their notes, ask them to move back to their original seats.

MAKE IT PERSONAL

- This week's study could be confusing for girls. Be sure to emphasize that walking away wisely does not mean holding on to old grudges and denying forgiveness. However, when a friendship is no longer healthy, it may be time to create some distance. We can't do the healing for our friends, and with some space they may better be able to find the healing they need in Jesus.

- Share with the group about a time when you had to walk away from a friendship. Did you experience the guilt of walking away? Did you see any transformation in that friend's life after you stepped out of the way?

BEFORE YOU GO

- Remind girls to finish the homework days on their own.

- Close by praying for your group. Ask the Lord to give girls strength and knowledge in their friendships. Pray that He would strengthen them to love their friends as He loves them and give them the knowledge to know when they are carrying too much for the sake of their friends.

WEEK 7

GET STARTED (OPTIONAL)

- Give every girl a blank piece of paper and a pen or pencil. Ask girls to draw a self-portrait and include one unknown fact about themselves at the bottom of the paper. Do not let girls peek at each others' drawings. Collect all of the portraits and try to guess each person's portrait together.

MAKE IT PERSONAL

- Since this is your last week together, consider meeting in a different location or going to dinner as a group.

- Ask girls to take time to reflect on the places you have been and the lessons you have learned during this study. Girls have opened up their hearts and grown together as a group. Together, spend some time considering ways they can be friends this week and dare to go first.

- As you work through this final week together, share how you have seen God working in your relationships during this study. Don't forget to include the ones that have formed as a result of your time together. Encourage girls to also share how this study has changed their own relationships.

BEFORE YOU GO

- Close by praying for your group. Pray for the friendships that the girls have cultivated over the past seven weeks. Thank God for all of the growing and sharing that has occurred in each girl. Ask God to help each girl be able to take what she has learned about friendships into all of her future relationships.

- Connect with girls during the week to remind them that you are praying for them even after your study has finished.

SOURCES

WEEK 1

1. Charles John Ellicott, *Ellicott's Commentary for English Readers* (1905), accessed February 10, 2017, accessed via https://www.studylight.org/commentaries/ebc/john-17.html#bibliography.

2. H. R. Reynolds and T. Croskery, *The Pulpit Commentary: John*, eds. H.D.M. Spence and Joseph S. Exell, accessed via mywsb.com.

3. Dietrich Bonhoeffer, *Life Together: The Classic Exploration of Christian in Community*, (New York: Harper & Row, 1954), 99.

4. Merrill C. Tenney and Richard E. Longenecker, *Expositor's Bible Commentary, Vol. 9: John and Acts*, ed. Frank E Gaebelein (Grand Rapids: Zondervan, 1981), accessed via mywsb.com.

5. Ibid.

6. Ibid., John 2:11.

7. Ibid., John 11:14-15.

WEEK 2

1. Kenneth L. Baker, ed., *NIV Study Bible* (Grand Rapids: Zondervan, 2008), accessed via mywsb.com.

2. Kenneth O. Gangel, *Holman New Testament Commentary: John*, ed. Max Anders (Nashville: Broadman & Holman, 2000), accessed via mywsb.com.

3. Timothy Keller, *The Freedom of Self Forgetfulness: The Path to True Christian Joy* (Leland, UK: 10Publishing, 2012), 44.

4. Clinton E. Arnold, ed., *Zondervan Illustrated Bible Backgrounds Commentary: Matthew, Mark, Luke, Vol. 1*, (Grand Rapids: Zondervan, 2002), accessed via mywsb.com.

5. "Roman Imperial Theology and the Gospel," *York College*, accessed March 7, 2017, http://york.edu/fewheel/John/Powerpoints/Roman%20Imperial%20Theology.pdf.

6. Arnold, *Zondervan Illustrated Bible Backgrounds Commentary*, accessed via mywsb.com.

7. Rodney A. Whitacre, *The IVP New Testament Commentary Series: John*, ed. Grant R. Osborne, (Downers Grove: InterVarsity Press, 1999) accessed via mywsb.com.

8. Ibid.

WEEK 3

1. Priscilla Shirer, *Fervent: A Woman's Battle Plan for Serious, Specific, and Strategic Prayer* (Nashville: B&H Publishing, 2015), 57.

2. Henry Cloud and John Townsend, *Safe People: How to Find Relationships That Are Good for You and Avoid Those That Aren't* (Grand Rapids: Zondervan, 1995), 65-66.

3. Dan B. Allender and Tremper Longman III, *Bold Love* (Colorado Springs: NavPress, 1992), 291.

4. Timothy Keller, "Adoration: Hollowed Be Thy Name," *Gospel in Life*, April 30, 1995, sermon, 30:10, accessed via gospelinlife.com/adoration-hallowed-be-thy-name-6391.

5. Cloud and Townsend, *Safe People*, 65.

6. Ibid., 65.

7. Joe Rigney, "When Envy Turns Deadly," *Desiring God*, blog, April 16, 2014, http://www.desiringgod.org/articles/when-envy-turns-deadly.

8. Henry H. Halley, *Halley's Bible Handbook with the New International Version, 25th ed.* (Grand Rapids: Zondervan, 2007), accessed via mywsb.com.

9. Chad Brand, Charles Draper, and Archie England, eds. *Holman Illustrated Bible Dictionary* (Nashville: Holman Bible Publishers, 2003), accessed via mywsb.com.

WEEK 5

1. Daniel Goleman, *Social Intelligence: The New Science of Human Relationships* (New York: Bantam Books, 2006), 11.

2. D. A. Carson, Walter W. Wessel, and Walter L. Liefield, *Expositor's Bible Commentary, Vol. 8: Matthew, Mark, Luke*, ed. Frank E Gaebelein (Grand Rapids: Zondervan, 1984), accessed via mywsb.com.

3. Ibid.

4. Daniel Goleman, *Social Intelligence*, 308.

5. Ibid.

6. Beth Moore, *Get Out of That Pit: Straight Talk about God's Deliverance* (Nashville: Thomas Nelson, 2007), 31.

7. Ibid., 33.

8. Ibid.

9. Ibid., 31.

10. Ibid., 33.

11. Goleman, *Social Intelligence*, 308.

WEEK 6

1. Kenneth L. Baker, ed. *NIV Study Bible* (Grand Rapids: Zondervan, 2008), accessed via mywsb.com.

2. Ibid.

3. *HCSB Study Bible* (Nashville: Holman Bible Publishers, 2010), accessed via mywsb.com.

4. Ibid.

5. Cloud and Townsend, *Safe People*, 97.

6. Ibid., 189.

7. Ibid., 189-190.

8. Ibid., 190.

9. Oswald Chambers, *My Utmost For His Highest* (Grand Rapids: Discovery House, 2010), https://books.google.com/books?id=drGWCgAAQBAJ&printsec=frontcover&source=gbs_ge_summary_r&cad=0#v=onepage&q&f=false.

10. Cloud and Townsend, *Safe People*, 197.

11. Ibid., 72-73.

12. Ibid., 199.

13. Ibid., 190-199.

14. Ibid., 197-198.

GIRLS MINISTRY RESOURCES

All Things New
By Kelly Minter

Over 8 sessions, Kelly Minter will lead girls through the Letter of 2 Corinthians to discover how Paul's encouragement to the believers in Corinth challenges the church and young women today. This Bible study also includes leader helps and 7 weeks of personal study to be completed between group sessions. As new creations in Christ, we are to spread the message of Jesus' grace, comfort, and generosity with the world. In the way we live, we must boldly declare that He makes all things new.

Student Book 005787455 $12.99

Worthy Vessel
By Amy Byrd

This six-session resource will lead girls through an in-depth study of 2 Timothy. They will examine biblical context and a multitude of spiritual truths in this letter from the apostle Paul to Timothy. As they explore the relationship between Paul and his young disciple, girls will be challenged to live as worthy vessels of the gospel of Jesus Christ, encouraging others to walk in faith as they deliver the message God has entrusted to them.

Student Book 006104413 $11.99
Downloadable Student eBook 005789762 $11.99
Leader Kit 006104400 $59.99
Digital Leader Kit 005792206 $59.99

Looking for Lovely
By Annie F. Downs

This seven-session study for middle-and high-school girls will challenge them to look for the lovely in the midst of trials. It is also designed to help girls persevere through those trials and grow in godly character and hope. Girls will study examples throughout the Bible of people who sought out the lovely in the midst of their everyday lives.

Student Book 005781390 $11.99
Downloadable Student eBook 006104392 $11.99
Digital Video Bundle 005788239 $24.99

Authentic Love
By Amy-Jo Girardier

Speaking directly to the hearts of young women, *Authentic Love: Christ, Culture, and the Pursuit of Purity* exposes culture's distorted messages about purity and love and reveals how God has created us for a lifestyle of personal holiness. Over the course of 8 sessions, girls will examine five attributes of holiness that shape our identity. They will be challenged to reject the self-serving influences of culture and embrace what it means to live as godly young women who reflect the character of Christ.

Girls Bible Study 005791915 $12.99
Girls eBook 005791916 $12.99
Girls Digital Leader Kit 005792342 $49.99

LifeWay STUDENTS

TO LEARN MORE OR PURCHASE, VISIT LIFEWAY.COM OR VISIT YOUR LOCAL LIFEWAY CHRISTIAN STORE.